The Power of Real E

The Seven Steps to Make Money & Create a Lifetime of Wealth

Kemi Egan

FREEDOM
PUBLISHING HOUSE

Published by Freedom Publishing House 2015

All of the information in this book is for informational purposes only. It is not nor is it intended to be advice or instruction. The author is not a qualified financial or legal advisor. The author, publisher, nor any person, company, nor entity make any warranty as to the appropriateness of this information for you or your situation. Like all of us, you take full responsibility for your actions, including seeking appropriate guidance and counsel from qualified individuals before taking any actions.

If you have any questions or would like to get in touch please visit:

www.freedomacademies.com

I'M HERE TO HELP

Whatever your goals and dreams if you just commit to the process, they can be yours. But you can't do it alone. When I was writing this book I knew I had more training, more tips and much more value I could give you than we could ever get in one book. So, I've created a community of like-minded people all out there striving to create wealth and build a future with real estate. So access your free membership and you'll get all the guides and support materials you can use to put everything in this book into action. I want to give you this free membership as a thank you for buying this book.

So, come and join the community and get INSTANT ACCESS to:

- **Free VIP Membership** to Freedom Property Academy (**http://www.freedompropertyacademy.com/book**)
- **Free Video training** from Kemi featuring joint venture training, real estate strategy training, audio and video programs supporting all 7 steps updated regularly. A comprehensive set of modules and resources online.
- **Attend Live Training webinars** from Kemi and the team. Updates will be posted inside the community for the latest training events where you can grab a hot seat.
- **Join the Community –** Post questions, help others and get joint venture opportunities, joint venture partners and access to VIP only events
- **Downloads and Resources –** Get access to documents, templates and examples from all seven modules. Joint venture presentation proformas, deal structuring examples and much, much more.

ONE MORE THING

I wrote this book for you. This is the book I would have loved during the first few years of my journey. I would love to hear what you think so if you leave a review on Amazon, Audible or anywhere else send me a link or screenshot at **kemi.egan@freedomacademies.com** and I have another extra special gift to thank you.

Thank You

The words are mine, but the experiences, the journey, and the laughs are ours, Laura. Thank you for being the best business partner and best friend ever! Your courage, strength, and damn spread sheets have changed lives.

The unwavering support and belief from our families has made everything possible. Thank you for your love and encouragement throughout the journey as we tried to change our lives and help others to do the same.

To everyone we have met and are yet to meet: You teach us so much and trust us with your hopes and dreams. We don't take that lightly and appreciate it more than you will ever know. We carry a piece of each of you with us as we try to break new ground to show you the path just as others have shown us the path.

In a generation of great change, we have had great leaders and teachers. They have shown us what can be achieved with a vision, courage, and determination. Brian Tracy, Mark Anastasi, Tony Robbins, Richard Branson, Karren Brady, Deborah Meaden, Robert Kiyosaki, Jeff Walker, Frank Kern, Brendon Burchard, Timothy Ferris, Warren Buffet, Robert G Allen, Queen Rania, Gandhi and so many more than I could ever fit on a page, thank you.

Contents

Introduction **1**

Down and Out 2

Trust the Process 4

Chapter One: The Wealth Mindset **6**

Roadblock One: Ignore everyone around you to protect your dream 7

Roadblock Two: Fail Forward 12

Roadblock Three: Know Your Why 13

Roadblock Four: Can you taste and smell success? 15

Roadblock Five: The procrastination curse 17

The 4 C's of Inaction 18

Chapter Two: The Wealth Map – Where are YOU? **27**

Instant Gratification 31

Strategy One: Pay Yourself First 32

Strategy Two: Take Control 35

Strategy Three: We're All Creatures of Habit 38

Chapter Three: Step Three :The Wealth Map-Where are you going?41

Plan 41

Keeping the Lights On 46

Strategic Wealth 50

Give Yourself a Pay Raise 51

Chapter Four: Step Four: Real Estate as Your Wealth Strategy **53**

Why You Should Be Investing in Real Estate 53

You Make Your Money When You Buy 54

Cash Flow Strategies 57

Cash Flow Strategy 1: Buy To Let 58

Cash Flow Strategy 2: Shared Houses 61

Multi-Let Success Blueprint 63

6 Essential Steps to Cash Flow Investments 68

Capital Growth/Gain Strategies 79

Chapter Five: Step Five: And Now to Turbo Charge 99

Focus 99

Up your game 100

80:20 Set and Forget 102

Front Load your Mistakes 105

Multiple Streams of Income 105

Business Income 107

Earned Income 108

Leveraged Income 110

Hands-Free Income 111

Sacrifice—Is It Worth It? 112

Chapter Six: Step Six Partnerships 114

Cash Joint Venture 117

Confidence Versus Competence 118

People Buy from People 120

Experience/Skills Joint Venture 122

Get a Partnership 'Through not To' 125

Pitching for Partners....127
Where Do You Meet Joint Venture Partners?....127
How to Avoid Bad Joint Venture Partners....133
P.O.W.E.R Joint Venture Model....135
Habits of the Wealthy....137
FEAR....139

Chapter Seven: Step Seven: Leverage Everything, Leverage Now ..143

Leverage People....144
Leverage Finance....146

About the Author....151

Introduction

"Real estate investing doesn't work. I knew this guy once, and he lost thousands buying this plan flat in the middle of nowhere, well hundreds of thousands probably. It nearly bankrupted him. The developer was corrupt, the attorneys were useless, and it all went wrong! Nope, no way. Real estate investing is not for me. Far too risky!"

Sound familiar?

If you have even a vague interest in real estate or have eyes and ears, at some point the subject of property investing will have come up in conversation with family and friends or colleagues. Maybe you mentioned that you you'd like to have a try at buying, refurbishing, and selling a house (also called *flipping*), or you've heard that you could use your own home to make some money and maybe buy a bigger house for your family. More than likely, you will have immediately been shot down by a 'Debbie Downer' and subjected to a thirty-minute monologue on the perils of real estate investing, swiftly followed by examples from *Make Money on your House in Thirty Seconds* or some other garbage TV show.

It might surprise you, but I agree with them. The fact is, they're right. You absolutely *can* lose a lot of money if you buy or invest in real estate without knowing what you're doing. Fact.

Conversely, you can absolutely make a *LOT* of money in a relatively short amount of time if you are educated, strategic, and well-positioned.

I should know. I have, I did, and I still do.

I'll talk about my personal journey throughout the book, but the short version is that when I began my real estate investing journey, I was homeless. My business partner and I were physical therapists. We met in college and decided we wanted to make a difference in health care. We wanted it to be top quality with brilliant therapists but still be accessible and affordable. But there was a small glitch in our plan. We were both excellent therapists, we traveled with national teams and were recruited by the top sports clubs, and we were paid to consult at other practices on how they could do things better—and we were only in our early 20s! We were young, energetic, and gifted. So what was the glitch? Well, we were terrible at business. Really, really awful. We didn't know the first thing about it, and worse than that, we didn't even think it mattered! We had a great clinic and happy customers. Surely that's all we needed, right? Umm, no! Very wrong. The problem was that we were in the middle of one of the biggest economic meltdowns the world had ever seen, and when money is tight, people tighten their belts, and the disposable income they have to spend shrinks significantly. So when you are focusing on keeping a roof over your head, things like a slightly stiff back or a sprained ankle suddenly plummet to the bottom of the list of things to which you allocate money to.

Down and Out

Being the naïve business owners we were, this didn't even cross our minds until it was too late. All of a sudden, the flow of clients dried up—as did the money in the bank. When the business started failing, it became apparent very quickly that it could no longer sustain our two apartments, and so we moved in together. It got rapidly worse because when businesses are in trouble, it requires strategic and talented business brains and leadership—which we were not—to find a solution. Before long, we had to move into our clinic and live in one room each. We showered in the council run leisure center across the road and ate whatever we could cook on a two-burner electric camping stove.

These were tough and dark times. I was living in a seventy square foot room with no windows and couldn't afford to see my family because they lived a few hundred miles away. I was too ashamed to tell them where I was living, partly because they couldn't afford to help and I didn't want them to worry and partly because of stupid pride. Even in those darkest days, I knew that I had something inside me that was meant for more. I always had the feeling that I was meant to change my life, the lives of my family, and the lives of thousands of other people. Even then, I still felt that fire burning inside me. I had no idea how it was going to happen, but I did know I wasn't done yet. This was just not my time!

After a few months of wallowing, giving in to my fear, and being lonely and depressed, I realized that there were millions of people around the world who had still managed to be successful. They were doing it—even in the recession—so there had to be a way. I figured if I could just hold on and figure out what all of these successful people knew that I didn't, I could finally claim the future designed for me.

So I set about reading every book I could get my hands on. I read about success, wealth, business, investing, mind-set, and real estate. I went to seminars and listened to podcasts. I devoured everything I possibly could in order to increase my knowledge and find the key.

Most people know the rest by now, the success story. They know that within twelve months of making that decision, I went from being homeless to having a portfolio worth over $2,000,000 and raising over $1,000,000 in joint venture finance. However, they don't know the entire struggle. Most people don't know I was up at 4 am twice a week in the early days to drive three and a half hours to an area where I knew the yields (cash returns) from buying real estate would be enough to increase my income substantially enough so we could move out—and I had no idea at the time how substantial that would be. They don't know that I went to a minimum of two networking meetings a week, even when I was so exhausted I was shaking. They don't know that I didn't pay a lot of my bills, sinking further into debt to pay for the gas and tickets to all of these events.

I'm not sharing this with you to impress you, but rather to implore you to take action. If I can do this, you can, too. I know you might be feeling confused or overwhelmed. I know that you're probably wondering if this is something that you can really do. If you're honest with yourself, you might feel like you really don't know how this is going to happen. Imagining yourself being successful might just be too much at the moment. That's okay. It's completely natural. Just remember this is a journey. You can't expect to see your final destination in any journey—you just know that if you keep making the right decisions and moving forward, you will get there.

That's all I'm asking of you right now. Trust in me. Trust in the process.

Trust the Process

This book will fill in the blanks and connect the dots for you. Most of the feedback I've received from members of the Freedom Property Academy community is that the actual strategies are the easy bits to learn. The fundamentals of lease options or the multi-let success blueprint or flips are actually straightforward, but most people get caught up on the processes. They find that the really challenging part is to understand and implement the strategic aspects. How do you position yourself as an expert when you don't have any experience? How can you get past objections? Those members are right—the tactical part is easy. It's the strategic insight, the knowledge you only gain from experience, that makes the difference. My first year in real estate was massive, but if I had known the real strategies I'm going to cover in this book, I would have blown the roof off it!

As a result, I'm going to address all of those questions, thoughts, and doubts here and provide you with as much clarity as I can so that you can get out there and get started. I'm going to share all of the things that it took me years to figure out—and that I wish I had known when I got started. It will be the difference between knowing a strategy and bumbling along or turbo-charging your results in a way that makes your income increase exponentially, completely changing your life in ways you can't even imagine.

The Power of Real Estate Investing

Before we get started, there's one more thing I would like to share with you…

Real estate investors often don't have great reputations. Like used car salesman, we get a really bad rap. The media, with a little help from some unscrupulous individuals, has portrayed us as money-grubbing, rip-off merchants always out to make a quick buck. The reality is that most investors I know are brilliant people. They provide quality homes, they look after their properties and their tenants, and they are fair and kind. They stop people from being foreclosed on, and they provide jobs and homes and much-needed investment in communities.

If you are just looking to get rich quickly, please put this book down and search the internet for some super-duper get-rich-quick tool that not even the experts know about yet that will make you four squillion dollars in thirty-five seconds for just one small upfront payment. If, however, you want to serve the world, provide great homes, add value and create jobs, do work you are proud of, and make a brilliant living, please read on. We need more of you.

Here we go…

Chapter One

Step One: The Wealth Mindset

Real estate investing is actually pretty straightforward. It doesn't require a degree in astrophysics from Harvard or the ability to code like Rain Man, and it doesn't require that you were born with a silver spoon in your mouth. That's one of my very favorite things about it—and about money in general. It doesn't care who you are, and it doesn't care about your background. Real estate is simply about strategically and tactically applying a number of strategies in order to add value. Whether you do a $10,000 refurbishment or use an educated financial strategy, you are taking a person or property from a place of low value to a place of high value and profiting along the way.

If you create massive value, wealth will flow to you.

There is a myth that the wealthy people are the big consumers in an economy and go around shopping and wasting money. Actually, the wealthiest are the *producers*. Look at the numbers. If you do one $10,000 refurbishment per year and sell a house for $27,000 more than you bought it for, you might earn $17,000 profit. But if you do five $10,000 refurbishments, you could earn $85,000. Producers provide more value, more service, and more products than they consume, and that is why they are so wealthy. If you're wondering why you're not where you want to be financially, ask yourself this: How much value have you added to how many people this year?

If you're honest, you've probably had some ideas of how to add value. You've thought about a business idea or a product that is needed but not out there yet. Maybe you saw a property for sale and thought you could do a great job fixing that up and then selling it. When it comes down to it, though, you don't do it. There are some very strategic and very simple ways to transform your life and attain wealth through real estate, all of which millionaire investors know about, and many of which we'll discuss in this book.

But there are also a couple of things you should know about which will guarantee you *don't* achieve the wealth you should and *don't* get to live the lifestyle you dream about. Things that stop you from achieving wealth are called roadblocks. No matter what you read, try, or think about, these things will come up time and again, so we're going to deal with them here once and for all so you are free to go out there, add value, and make a fortune.

Roadblock One: Ignore everyone around you to protect your dream

Since the financial crisis was dropped on our doorstep, the world has been in a state of perpetual confusion. The vast majority of people don't know whether to be optimistic, scared, excited, or nervous about the future. And depending on which newspaper you read on any given day (and I strongly suggest you don't read any), it will generally sway your personal views on the state of the world and whether you have a good or a bad day. It really is that dramatic and ridiculous—in equal measures.

The majority of the world wakes up, checks their smart phone, and then reads the paper or listens to the news—all of which is invariably negative. Let's be honest, the media never has anything good to say except for maybe the occasional blurb about a giant panda giving birth. It's depressing. And while you can probably see through all the nonsense, propaganda, and agenda, unfortunately your friend down at the bar can't—nor will 95% of everyone you speak to throughout the day. So the world is full of people running around and believing the garbage, gradually filling your head with the negative nonsense that will become the basis of your decisions.

There is a direct correlation between consumer spending and reported news. For example, when news breaks that a company may be firing their CEO, the shares plummet. Often, this is all speculation, but who has benefited? All the folks that bought their shares that day and the Wall Street banks that trade them. Here's another example—when the papers report that the recession isn't over and jobs are at risk, what happens? People stop spending and investing because they're scared. They start leaving their money in the bank, getting a measly 1% per year. And who benefits? The banks and their shareholders. How? Well, the banks are only allowed to invest a certain percentage of the amount they have deposited. So if Bank A has $5m deposited by customers like you, they then take that money and invest it or lend it out in order to make themselves *more* money. However, due to the rules that regulate the financial industry, they may be legally allowed to invest/lend out only 20% of that to earn more money. So when the sun is shining, and we are all being offered 5—15% on various investments, we withdraw our funds to start getting a better return on our money, which is great news for us. But if 50% of us withdraw 50% of our funds, the amount the banks have in the kitty and are therefore allowed to invest is significantly reduced, and they lose money.

This book isn't about conspiracy theories or drama, but the fact is that there are a lot of people with a lot of ulterior motives and agendas that don't have anything to do with what is best for *you*. Your role is to block out all of that noise and nonsense so you can focus on the things you can control to create wealth for your family.

Imagine the impact that filling your head with positivity would have on your day and on your decisions!

What if you were able to go about your day and be totally oblivious to all of the negative messages, the ones that constantly seek to penetrate your mind and affect your decisions? Just remember, everyone is trying to sell you something, but it is your role to decide if and how well that product serves you and your family.

When you begin to create wealth and change your life, there will be people who are unsettled by it. That's just life. You see, humans by their very nature use each other as a kind of measuring stick, a ruler to measure themselves and gauge their progress by. When you begin to make changes in your life, it invariably forces those around you to take a look at their own lives. They start thinking about whether or not they are truly happy, whether they are achieving everything they want. For around 98% of the population, this self-evaluation is scary. It's simply too scary to peep above the parapet and actually evaluate things for what they really are, so they begin to put you down or knock your dreams and ideas. It's not because they don't believe you can achieve them, but more likely because they believe you *will*—and that will affect how they measure themselves with that invisible ruler.

When the negativity starts—and you know the kind of thing I mean, 'Don't be so silly,' 'You could never…,' 'Haven't you seen the papers? The banks aren't lending,' or maybe even 'You are out of your mind! Who would invest money in you?'—don't take it personally. Let all of that negativity right out the back door. There is no room in your mind for this kind of stuff. As it stands, you are already trying to juggle your full-time job, your family, and maybe your kids and their millions of after school clubs. No matter what occupies your time, your plate is full, and you need to save all the space you can for your pursuit of an ethical and sustainable wealth for yourself and your family—and in order to give something back to the world.

I wish someone had shared this with me in the early days of my investing career. When you have new valuable knowledge and skills, you're desperate to share it with anyone who will listen. You're so excited about this knowledge you have—knowledge that you know will change people's lives—that you want to shout it from the rooftops. But whereas you, I, and others in our community immerse ourselves in education and mastery and strive for a success built on positivity, drive, and determination, those on the outside aren't necessarily of the same mind-set or on the same track. As a result, they will reflect onto you their negativity. So as you announce a new strategy and try to explain it, they will listen and then immediately bounce back to you all of the reasons why it won't work.

Protect your dreams ferociously and don't be swayed. Your future is too important. Be careful with whom you share your dreams. Find yourself a team—a tribe of people all pulling together in the same direction, aiming for the same things. You'll be surprised at how quickly those around you who had previously been negative will come around once they start seeing you succeed!

In the meantime, you need to develop blinders. You need to be able to filter out information and feedback from the people who have no idea what they're taking about but accept support and advice from anyone who has been there and done it.

This was a lesson that took me a good few years to learn. I would attend mentoring sessions, taking advice and guidance from millionaires—many times over—and then going home to put it all into action. Always, I would seek approval and validation from a friend or family member, asking what they thought. Almost without fail, I'd suddenly be confronting a 'Debbie Downer' who would tell me I was all wrong. Between then and the next mentoring session, I'd tie myself in knots not knowing which way was up or who I should be listening to. At my next session, my mentor would smile knowingly—annoyingly—and just ask, "Kemi, when was the last time Auntie Betty (or whomever) made a million dollars from real estate investing?" The answer was, of course, never. Second question—"Kemi, is Auntie Betty your target market?" The answer was, of course, *no*.

The lesson from all this? Ignore anyone who hasn't been there and done what you're trying to do many times over! If you're still not sure let the market tell you. The market will bite or not bite. People will either buy, or they won't buy, and they'll go elsewhere. But your friend at the local bar is neither your mentor nor your market. If you still want to spend time with him, go ahead and order a drink, but change the subject! Don't allow your financial future to be dictated to you by the Debbie Downers of the world and those too scared to even try to reach for the future that is rightfully theirs.

Here's another angle—your friends and family love you. They would do anything in their power to prevent you coming to any harm. The notion that you want to create wealth and change your life is terrifying to them because unless they've been with you on the journey to this point, they won't have the same knowledge and skills that you have to help you create wealth. Even if you've only read one book or listened to one podcast, you're still a couple of steps ahead of them already—and those are the biggest steps. Your mind is open to possibility, and you've realized that your past doesn't need to reflect your future. You suddenly view the world like a child with eyes wide open in awe.

When you share these dreams with your family, they envision you being hurt, let down, and disappointed because it's just 'not realistic.' To them, the thought of failure is so scary it's not even worth the chance that you might succeed. That isn't a reflection on you, or on how good they think you are—that is just how we are trained to think. From an early age at school, we are taught that being wrong is bad and failing is negative, and so we enter our adult lives carrying this baggage with us. Because of this, your family might not be as excited for you as you'd hoped. They might even be actively trying to discourage you. But rather than becoming frustrated or downhearted, it's important to remember that they are just scared for you. Love them unconditionally, enjoy them, and remember they want the best for you—but protect your dreams and ignore the naysayers.

You want to create wealth for yourself and your family, you want the means to protect and secure their future, and that is far too important to quit on merely because they—and you—are scared. I was scared. I made decisions to spend money on education when I couldn't even pay my credit card bill and was at risk of being evicted from the clinic we were sleeping in—the only roof over my head. Every self-made millionaire I have ever met was scared at some point, but for us, and for you, the fear of things *not* changing, the fear that we may never achieve all we are capable of, is far more terrifying.

Roadblock Two: Fail Forward

Failure is not fatal, but fear is paralyzing.

For most of us, failure is a chronic condition that has connotations of misery, negativity, and disappointment. If we believe everything we are told, failure is catastrophic and fatal. But to most millionaires, failure is a daily occurrence. The difference is we call it a learning experience. If you try something new, the chances are you'll fail at it a few times first. Do you remember learning to drive? Thinking that trying to check mirrors, change gears, and turn left all at the same time was impossible? What about the next time you buy a new car, and the bite point for the clutch is all different, so you stall the car the first time out? Is that failing? Do you stop trying and decide to walk everywhere instead?

The legendary Jim Rohn was a millionaire by age thirty-one and then lost it all a couple of years later. So is it success for achieving vast wealth in the first place? Or failure for then losing it all? Incidentally, Jim went on to create that wealth again in half the time because he had the skills, and his temporary setback didn't take those skills away from him.

Chances are if you haven't failed very much, you actually haven't succeeded very much, either. Rather than being polar opposites, success and failure are both ends of the same continuum. To succeed at anything, you have to keep trying and failing until you succeed. The amazing thing about human nature is that once we've developed that skill and can do it, we usually try it again. It will be a quicker, shorter, and better path the next time, but again we might fail. The faster you fail and start again, the faster you can achieve your dreams.

Use failure as motivation to keep trying.

If there are four possible ways of doing something, but only one is the right way, you wouldn't stop doing it just because you happened upon the wrong path the first time. Of course not! Because now the odds are in your favor. There are only two more times—*maximum*—that you can be wrong before you succeed. BOOM!

Get your head around it now. You *will* mess up. You *will* say something that sounds stupid, and in a few years you might well look back and cringe. But here's the thing—if you don't learn what *not* to say, how will you ever know what *to* say?

There are a million things that you can possibly mess up, but remember that you are coming at real estate investing from a place of wanting to help and wanting to make a difference in the world while at the same time earning a great living, so if you say the wrong word or get the paperwork wrong during a visit to a homeowner, but you stop them from being foreclosed on, do you think they will care? *Hell no!*

Each and every time you fail, bounce onward because you've just narrowed the odds of your success.

Roadblock Three: Know Your Why

Why do you want wealth? The journey to wealth is exciting and challenging. It brings you experiences and personal growth that you didn't know existed, and often the journey is not easy. So I ask you again, why do you want to achieve wealth?

For some people the *why* is the latest luxury car, and for others it's the opportunity to have a voice and be heard. Many will say they want wealth to protect and secure their family or to set up a charity foundation and make a difference in the world. Sometimes it's a combination of all of the above!

The reason you want to achieve wealth is a deeply personal one, and it speaks to the very core of you. Whatever it is, make sure you want it more than anything else. It must be powerful enough to keep you going when times are hard and get you out of bed when the mornings are dark and the sun hasn't yet risen. No self-made person will tell you that the journey to wealth is all rainbows and butterflies, but they will tell you that when you have clarity of vision, when you know your true north, and when you allow nothing to deviate you from the course, the journey is magical. It will lead you to places and people you could never have imagined possible. Don't be surprised as you continue along the journey to see your *why* change and evolve as you do.

Donald Trump said, "If you're going to think, you may as well think big." This is vital as you reflect upon your motivation, your reason for doing this. It's very tempting to allow our logical brain to try and make sense of our dreams and process them in a way we can understand. This isn't the time for logic. At this stage, all we need to know is where we are going and what the first step is. When you get in your car to go somewhere, you don't always know exactly what lies before you. You don't know which lights will be red or where there will be traffic. You know only your destination, and that you have to take the journey one road at a time.

The power of your *why* will get you through the difficult, the mundane, the laborious, and the boring. It will get you up in the morning and keep you working late into the night.

Your *why* will come from what you believe to be true and what you believe to be worth the struggle Logically, if you're a millionaire, and I offer you $50,000 to face your greatest fear, you probably wouldn't do it. If I asked the same question again, but this time it was to save their child, they would be there with bells on. The difference? Their core values told them that although the risk and fear was just as great the reward was worth it.

People are either motivated toward something or away from something. You might be motivated to achieving a portfolio of ten properties or you might be motivated away from looking silly for wasting time and money on books and education and not doing anything about it. Ultimately, it doesn't really matter whether you are motivated by the stick or the carrot as long as that is enough for you to keep on keeping on.

I had a very specific motivation for a long time. When I was around thirteen years old, a teacher asked me one day—in front of the class—what I wanted to be when I grew up. I answered, "The best physical therapist in the world" to which she snorted and laughed then retorted, "Kemi, if you're lucky, you will be a cleaner or a criminal." I was heartbroken. She had, in one whimsical statement, crushed me. For years, one of my biggest motivations was proving her wrong. I wanted so badly for her to see me as the person I could be. This wasn't exactly an honorable goal, and for a long time I felt bad about it, but many of my mentoring clients feel the same way.

Not all of your goals have to be altruistic or about saving the planet. As long as it isn't illegal or immoral, be motivated by whatever moves you. Our enemies help us to stand tall with pride and fight with conviction. This power shouldn't be underestimated. It should instead be harnessed and to fuel us.

When you want to succeed as much as you want to breathe, then you'll be successful. Eric Thomas

Roadblock Four: Can you taste and smell success?

Vision Boards

A vision board is a fantastic way to help you keep your dream close to you and keep you moving forward when times are challenging.

If you haven't seen them before, vision boards are sheets of paper covered in pictures and words that illustrate your goals and dreams. Vision boards are incredibly powerful because humans think in pictures.

Try it now. Imagine a Hawaiian beach. Did you see the words *clear blue sea, golden beaches, sun beating down*? Or did you imagine standing ankle deep in beautiful, warm waters with the waves lapping at your ankles and the sun beating down on your shoulders? Pictures, right? So when you are coming up with your goals, you need to engage that part of your brain. Written goals are great, but visual goals in pictures are incredible!

You can do this on your computer or on a sheet of paper, but you need to immerse yourself in a search for pictures of cars, vacations, friends, adventures, theaters, ski trips, dolphins, a great office, you being healthy and happy. Put earnings or a net worth on whatever it is that you want out of your life—anything that gets you excited and motivated. Then have your online document printed in full color—try eBay for a massive poster that costs a couple of bucks. I recommend that you also get a small one as well that you can have on you at all times. Imagine how powerful it will feel to literally carry your dreams around with you wherever you go. Whenever you feel a little bit overwhelmed or maybe even want to quit, just pull out your dreams and look at them. Imagine the sounds, the tastes, the feelings. And ask yourself again if you are ready to quit.

After a while, you won't even need to look at the paper. Just the feel of it against your hand when you put your hand in your pocket will be enough to lift your mood, strengthen your determination, and put a smile on your face.

The human brain can't distinguish between your imagination and reality. Hundreds of studies have been carried out on athletes and high performers. Researchers placed electrodes on the head and muscles of test subjects, using them to monitor electromagnetic responses. Simply put, they wanted to measure any electrical activity, any sign of neurons firing up. Without fail, when the researchers asked the athletes to imagine their sport—running a 100m race, for example—not only do the same parts of their brain fire up as when they are actually running, but they have the same muscular response. The muscles in their arms and legs not only fire up, but they do it in the same order and manner that they do when actually performing the action. That's incredibly powerful.

If you apply that to your goals and your life, your body literally prepares for success—as if it was actually happening. You are strengthening your powers of success and performing at the highest level just by thinking about it. This action alone can help you make the shift from hoping and vaguely wishing to being present and focused in the moment.

Roadblock Five: The procrastination curse

You've known for a while that you're meant for something more. You know that you're meant to be more, do more, have more, and give more. Even when the business was fantastic, and I was earning okay money, I knew that wasn't it for me. I always felt that I was the one who was supposed to look after my mom and give her the life she deserved and change things for my family. Deep down, there's been this burning desire inside you as well, a desire to have an amazing life full of love and laughter and experiences without the daily struggle of making ends meet. You also probably know that you can make a difference in the world. You know you have skills and talents and that people can relate to you and trust you. Given the chance, you could really do great things. But you haven't.

Before I knew there was any potential for me to invest in real estate (I used to think you needed money to do that), I was fascinated by it. I loved architecture, the concepts, the theories. I knew if I could just wiggle one of my little toes in the door, I could pry that door open and do some amazing stuff. I got loads of training, read hundreds of books, went to seminars and conferences, and listened to audios. I eventually found myself a great mentor, and I knew from within the deepest part of me that it was the right vehicle for me, for my passions, and for my journey. But I still didn't act on it right away.

At that time in the UK, we were building around 130,000 too few homes each year. We were around 1,000,000 homes short of where we needed to be. And with an increasing birth and divorce rate plus immigration, the housing situation was dire and was only getting worse. We needed—and still do need—educated, strategic, and disruptive investors and developers to go out and provide great homes and jobs to keep the economy moving through the next cycles. But I *STILL* didn't do anything.

So what was stopping me? And what's stopping you?

Think about it now. Why haven't you done anything? I'm not naïve enough to think this is the first or the last book on wealth or real estate you have or will ever read. So why haven't you acted? Likely, like I was, you are also immobilized, frozen, by the four C's of inaction.

Across all the people we've mentored here in the community you can identify four things that have stopped them moving forward. I'm going to spell them out for you here so when those voices creep into your mind, you recognize them. Like all irrational fears when you recognize them you can then acknowledge them and then drop kick them out of the back door so you keep moving forward.

The 4 C's of Inaction

Consumed

When you are caught up in day-to-day life, just trying to survive, it's difficult to see the wood through the trees. It's so easy to become consumed with the usual challenges you face every day that you lose sight of your *why*. It's easy to forget why you have taken on an extra workload, why you are spending what little time you have learning a new skill, taking a class, studying financial reports, creating systems and processes, or networking.

Retaining your *why* here is crucial. Take out your vision board and feel the excitement. Let the possibility wash over you. It's the difference between giving up and quitting on your dreams and getting the results you've always gotten or becoming part of the two percent who make the time, who create the luck, who stand firm, and who achieve their goals.

For a short time, you might need to reprioritize some things to give you the brain room and the time to pursue your investment career and wealth. I know this isn't sexy, but I promised you a real toolkit to help you make real money, not a get-rich-quick-with-no-work scheme. It will take work, and it might take time, but the results are more than worth it.

In the meantime, get technology on your side. There are some great tools I use that have helped me fight the feeling of being consumed. Tools sometimes help to free some time from running back and forth.

Some great tools I use to help the fight against being 'consumed':

www.scheduleonce.com

This is an online diary management system that allows other people to see your schedule, book meetings and conference calls with you, and stop the incessant back and forth of trying to arrange times. It even integrates with your phone calendar.

Email auto responder

I get hundreds of emails a day and, at one point, they were consuming me. Even the act of going through them to find the urgent ones that needed a reply took hours. It was overwhelming. After reading Tim Ferriss's book *The 4-Hour Workweek,* I set up an auto-responder that sends out an automatic response, saying, "Thank you for your email. I really appreciate it. I'll get back to you ASAP, but if it's really urgent, please forward your email to my PA (put her email). If you don't do that, I'll assume it isn't urgent. Have a great day." This small act enables me to stay on top of the urgent emails that need my attention and spend time replying to the other emails in my allotted diary time.

Diarizing

I'm not a natural diary person, so this took some to learn and practice, but now everything in my life is diarized—from the time I work out to when I hold weekly meetings with my team. I have specific days and times I do interviews and specific times I respond to emails. Although it seems very rigid, it's actually quite freeing. This gives me the opportunity to relax, safe in the knowledge that everything has its time. I don't have to worry that X—a contract with a developer, perhaps—will get read, or when I'll do it, because when I get to Wednesday PM, for example, I know that I read contracts that are due to be signed between 2 pm and 4 pm. When that time arrives, my PA will give me a pile of contracts to read, and that one will be in it. It helps me relax and focus on one thing at a time, and it also protects valuable time with my family as well. This little trick will ensure that you protect the time allocated for your wealth creation.

Capacity

The average brain can store about seven things in short-term memory before it starts struggling to keep up. In humans, reaching capacity takes the form of frustration, stress, and sometimes anger or even tears. When you have a lot going on in your life already, hitting capacity becomes increasingly common and damaging. One of the simplest ways to increase your brain capacity is to write lists. Carry a notebook or makes notes in your phone or tablet. Write down any thoughts, ideas, or to-dos that pop up in your head. This prevents you from trying to holding it all in your brain and feeling overwhelmed with how much you have to remember.

You have a great set of talents specific to you. There are some things at which you are amazing, and increasing your focus on those skills and talents will turbo charge your wealth at a speed you can't even imagine. But it will happen only if you allow yourself to do it. Wasting time trying to memorize lists is crazy. I work with so many people that a) tell me they're forgetful or b) brag about how much they can remember and the fact they don't need to write things down. Both types of people are going about things all wrong. It's natural to forget when your brain is juggling a hundred things, but that doesn't make you forgetful or not capable. Equally, relying on your memory will at some point let you down. So don't be afraid to write things down, no matter which type of person you are. I love the idea that in 100 years, someone will find a dusty box of my notebooks in the loft and be able to read my notes, my ideas, my theories. It's an exciting and unexpected legacy.

These are some great tools I use to help fight capacity overwhelm:

www.evernote.com - Your brain can only remember so many things at once, and this great tool enables you to sync all your notes, pictures, and reminders across all of your devices—you won't need to rummage through your phone, your tablet, and your computer for the note you made on a particular website. For a small fee, it also lets you collaborate with your team so that all of you can see where you are at a certain point point on any number of projects without adding more emails to your inbox.

www.moleskine.com - Gorgeous notebooks and diaries to make note of your thoughts and leave a stunning legacy.

Voice memos—Depending on your phone, you should be able to record voice memos. Perfect for when you are on the move and want to remember something. Even better when you have an idea that you can't quite articulate on paper—just talk into your phone and have the memory there when you need it.

Complexity

The truth is we all come with baggage. We have all been hurt, disappointed, and let down, and we carry that with us. When we are born, we're like diamonds—beautiful, exciting, and full of promise. We are optimistic about the world and the opportunities before us. Then as we go through school and grow up, we are told repeatedly we aren't good enough, that we have failed. Gradually, layer after layer of this mud covers us, and we no longer resemble that diamond. As we begin to work, get married, and go about our lives, we figure out that we need to put on a brave face. And so we then cover ourselves in a layer of shiny paint. For all external intents and purposes, we look shiny and new, but below those painted layers, we are struggling.

This whole process affects our decisions, our judgments, and how we see the world. It determines whether we bury our heads in the sand and ignore things or react angrily and become defensive. Our experiences form what we understand as truth. If you think about it, you can see it all around you. You know people who believe that everything will be alright in the end and that everything will figure itself out, and you also know people who, no matter what occurs, are always waiting for things to fail and expecting the worst. When you listen to them speak, you are hearing their belief system and their experiences of the world.

We are complex beings, and our brains have lots of different parts. One of those parts is known as the *reptile*. This part of us evolved from a time long ago, when humans dealt with much greater threats to our basic human needs—food, warmth, and shelter. Often times, when we're feeling stressed or angry, it's because the reptile within us is experiencing vulnerability. Take a moment at those times to analyze your surroundings and the present situation. Is something going on that may have triggered the fight or flight part of your brain? Often, by identifying that trigger, you will find yourself a lot calmer and then be able to process complex tasks. Depending on our baggage, we need to break our day down into very manageable pieces to keep our reptile happy. These should include eating healthily nutritious meals, staying hydrated, and taking five or ten minutes alone each day to process all of the input we have received.

As you become a more experienced business owner, real estate investor, and leader, you will find that the things that challenged you in the beginning are no longer an issue. The issue hasn't changed—you have. Read a book now, and then again in three years. You will see different points upon your second reading. The book hasn't changed, but *you* have.

I find it useful to score challenges in my notebook. I give them a number out of ten as a way of measuring how challenging I find them. For example:

Challenge	Score last year	Score now
Managing $5m development	5/10	2/10
Writing complaint emails	4/10	3/10
Finding time to exercise	8/10	6/10

The joy of this is that in a year, you can review your tables and score the challenges, watching the scores continue to drop as your emotional intelligence grows and your capacity to cope with complexity increases.

Mentors can be invaluable during this process. People who have been where you are and are now where you want to be can guide you and give you strategies they've used to cope with the demands and the transition in their life.

Confusion

Confusion looks a lot like fear. If we don't feel like we have enough information, or we don't understand the terminology, we don't feel like we can make an informed decision—and so we go right back to burying our head in the sand, wallowing in indecision. A deer caught in the headlights.

A great illustration of this is new drivers in an area they're unfamiliar with. You'll see them swerving between lanes, indicating they intend to turn one direction and then abruptly changing their mind. The famous saying in driving applies also to life: Indecision causes accidents.

The fantastic thing about decisions in business and real estate is that

99% of the time, any decision is the right decision. When you are making decisions regarding your financial future, most of the time you won't have 100% of the information you would like. A lot of your decisions will be based on your gut and your experience. Usually, we have enough information, and if we don't, we can get it quickly. But we can't make more time. Too much of life has been spent in struggle, and now it's time to act. Follow your training. Make decisions and make them fast. If you are wrong, be wrong fast. Get it out of the way and then make another decision. Procrastinating for two weeks won't change your chances of being right, but it will delay your moving forward. Be wrong often, and be wrong fast.

In my first year of real estate investing, I viewed a house that I was going to buy to rent out. It was a great house at a great price, but there were a couple of issues with the ownership title, and I felt like I needed more information and get it resolved before I moved on. Many people tried to assure me that things would be fine, but a lot of their advice was contradictory and confusing—and it scared me even more. In the end, I did nothing. Well, actually, I did do something—by failing to make a decision, I lost out on a great opportunity, and I wasted a couple of months and missed another opportunity whilst going back and forth on the original one. The truth is that buying it would have worked out, and if there was a problem, there was very little that the attorney couldn't have fixed. Not buying it would also have been fine. But doing neither cost me money and delayed my plans by months.

Fail fast. Fail often. Fail forward. Fail your way to success.

The rest of the steps in this book are going to detail the strategies and tools I used to completely transform my life and achieve stratospheric results in under a year. They are things that you can use as well. These are the same skills and strategies I've used to grow my wealth, my portfolio, and my businesses year to year. It's not because I'm a rocket scientist, but because success and failure leave footprints. Everyone who has ever achieved anything great has left clues and footprints pointing to how they did it, and by playing a little dot-to-dot, we can follow their paths and do the same. Really successful people are not only happy to fail—because as we now know, that's when you learn the most—but they are also happy to share what they've learned. Growing up, I had a favorite phrase— *I'll make my own mistakes.* Now, that's changed. If I can learn from *someone else's* mistakes and apply that to my life, I will. I want the shortcut to success!

This is a compilation of everything I've learned from reading thousands of books, going to hundreds of seminars, spending thousands and thousands of dollars on conferences, listening to numerous hours of audiobooks and podcasts and applying them to my life, and gaining years of experience and learnings. I have written the guide to making money through real estate that I wish I'd had to learn from when I began.

Making money, especially long term, sustainable, and ethical wealth does take work. It can be challenging. But there is a definite slow lane and fast lane to success and wealth. The slow lane is to try and figure things out all by yourself, to make your own mistakes and hope you stumble across a solution that has evaded you this far in your life.

Welcome to the fast lane.

Is it easy? Yes. There's no genius or mystique here. No smoke and mirrors or illusion. No teaching one thing and doing another.

Is it difficult? Yes. It requires commitment and conviction.

The easiest things to do are also the easiest things not to do. This time needs to be different for you. You owe it to yourself to stick with it, to follow the strategy I set out for you, and to finally get the results you and your family deserve.

Action Steps:

Commit to removing all the road blocks from your life and protecting your dreams.

Log in to your free membership area at
www.freedompropertyacademy.com/book

- Watch the Step one training videos
- Create your vision board
- Have it printed and carry it with you

Chapter Two

Step Two: The Wealth Map – Where are YOU?

The differentiating factor between humans and animals is *will.* Animals are driven by genetics and evolution. They sleep when it's dark and eat when they're hungry because that is instinctual for them. This is why people who have kept wild animals as household pets have often found that sooner or later, nature kicks in, and that 'pet' they have lovingly cared for and trained bites them—or worse. Not because they wanted to, but because it's their nature. Humans, unlike animals, have choice. We have thoughts, a conscience, a feeling of responsibility, and a will. Responsibility and will are incredible and powerful things. Responsibility will drive a parent to work three jobs to provide for his or her children. Responsibility will motivate a football player to play on with a broken bone because he is part of a team. Responsibility is what will make a CEO have sleepless nights and fight like a dog to protect his employees.

Human will is even more powerful. Harnessed and used correctly, it's an incredible thing. Human will kicks in when logic and physical and mental abilities aren't enough. There have been some incredible feats of human will, completely unexplainable by any other phenomenon.

- Women have been known to lift cars off of babies.
- Climbers can scale a sheer rock face with no ropes and no grips.
- Denise Lewis MBE won an Olympic gold medal in heptathlon at the Sydney Olympics with virtually every part of her body strapped and taped.
- Ultramarathon runners complete 7+ back-to-back marathons through the desert in searing heat.
- Aron Ralston chopped his own arm off with a blunt

penknife to survive when getting stuck in the desert.

We all have this capability inside of us, but it usually takes something dramatic for us to engage and use it. Usually the trigger is fear. When we are scared, a rush of hormones occurs, triggering the fight or flight mechanism which does literally what it says on the tin—it makes us fight for our life, or run the other way.

Right now, you are fighting for your life. It might not be a literal fight, but it's a fight for your heart, soul, and dreams. You are fighting for the right to grow old comfortably with pride and, most importantly, with no regrets. Right now, you are fighting for the opportunity to live the life you've dreamed about. And make no mistake—the fight is real.

Take ultimate responsibility.

"I can't afford to…"

"I don't have time to…"

"I don't know how to…"

"No one told me…"

"I would have, but…"

"It wasn't my fault…"

"I was late because…"

How many times a day do you find yourself saying things like these? One, two, five, ten? Chances are it's so engrained in your language that you don't even notice.

I was first introduced to the idea of personal responsibility in an enlightening, albeit terrifying, one-week period. I had begun reading a book, and a massive chapter was all about taking responsibility for everything that happens in your life. *EVERYTHING*. Being the wise fool I was in my early twenties, I decided that what I had just read absolutely couldn't be the case. I mean, not *everything* was my fault, right? I couldn't help it that there was a massive credit crunch, and no one was seeking out my business. This is what I told myself, and happily content that the author was wrong, I continued about my week.

At the end of that week, I happened to be booked into a two-day personal development seminar. I'd been reading books, I'd been to a few seminars, and I was probably a little cocky about this whole 'personal development' thing. I figured, one course and you were set. I told you I wasn't a genius! Luckily, I've learned a lot since then.

So there I was, financially screwed but thinking that it had nothing to do with me, and *BOOM*—there it was again. Day 2 of my seminar. *Everything that happens is your responsibility and therefore in your control right now.*

If you have the will.

Wherever you are standing right now, your life is giving you feedback from all the earlier decisions you have made. You see, our lives are a compilation of all of our habits, both good and bad. If we are carrying a little too much weight, it's easy to say, "I'm still carrying baby weight" or "I work so hard I don't have time to eat properly." In essence, we are saying that we have decided not to prioritize our health to ensure we get a great diet with lots of fruits and vegetables and exercise that raises our heart rate and strengthens our muscles. If every time we ate too much of something unhealthy, we instantly gained ten pounds, we would eat better for sure. But life doesn't give us feedback that quickly. The powerful thing here is that if we decided to focus our energy on our health, the weight would go. It is in our control, *if* we have the will.

If we aren't in the financial position we would like to be, it's easy to say, "My job doesn't pay me very well" or "I don't earn enough to invest" or "I'm rubbish with figures, and I have no idea where my money goes." When we say these things, what we are really saying is that we haven't done whatever it takes to create wealth and ensure our family is secure. We didn't have the will. Correcting these problems could mean taking a class to understand figures and learning about profit and loss, or it could be not having a daily beer to save a couple of dollars that you can use to invest. What if every time you wasted $5 or walked past an opportunity to create wealth, money literally dropped out of your wallet? Conversely, what if every time you made a great financial decision, your bank account numbers went up immediately, and your wallet grew a bit fatter? Do you think you might be in a different financial situation right now?

Absolutely yes. As humans, we like instant feedback. If we do something well, we like a pat on the back, and if we do something poorly, we like to be told right away so that we can adjust and not end up in the doghouse. Unfortunately, life doesn't give us instant feedback, but if you take the time to look around, you will see the feedback from all of the previous decisions you have made.

Before our lives can change, before we can step into the future that we truly deserve, we must 100% own those decisions. We must take full responsibility for what we have created. This doesn't mean you should beat yourself up or play the blame game. Just stand up, straighten up, and acknowledge that you did the best you could with what you had at the time, but from now on, things are going to be different. They are going to better.

You can have wealth or you can have excuses, but you can't have both.

This process is a scary one, just like the decision you've made to invest in real estate and become wealthy. However, when you realize that you have created everything you have around you—the good *and* the bad—you are in a position to create everything amazing you want, if you have the will. That's exhilarating and powerful.

Instant Gratification

Wealth is a combination of health, fulfilment, happiness, satisfaction, and yes, money, but it is far more than numbers on a bank statement.

Instant gratification is a disease that has afflicted humans in an increasingly destructive way over the last century. We have developed a perceived need to have everything we want, and have it right away, no matter whether we have earned it or if it's even good for us. Credit cards are an excellent example of this. They were created to make it quicker and easier to spend money on things we couldn't afford. Roll back in time fifty years. If you couldn't afford that new sofa, you had to save up or ask family for some extra money. This took time, effort, and energy. Before you went begging, cap in hand, to everyone you knew, you had to decide whether you really wanted—or needed—that sofa.

Before fast food, microwaves, and processed snacks, if you were hungry, you cooked some nutritious food that was natural, unprocessed, and full of vitamins and minerals. It not only eradicated your hunger, but it also gave you the energy to complete your daily routine. Cooking isn't a quick process, though, and it forced you to plan meals. When would you eat? What would you eat? Did you have enough food in the house for the week? Did you budget for enough meals? And then fast food came along. Spontaneous purchases. No thinking involved. Instant gratification.

At the beginning, when you're most likely creating wealth from a standing start, instant gratification will be your biggest enemy. Spur of the moment decisions will take all your extra money and time and will delay you attaining the true wealth you really deserve. If we want to have our own vineyard, we cannot chop off the branches and fruits as soon as they bud. We must wait for the bush to mature and become a fully-fledged tree in order to benefit from its produce for years to come.

When you landed your very first job, you more than likely went out and spent your first paycheck as soon you had it in your hand. It takes a while to realize that when you do that, you don't have anything left for the month, and so you then start to spread out your purchases, saving some of your money for later in the month. When you decide you want to buy a bike or a car or your first home, you need to try to master saving. Every decision becomes an exercise in bargaining and compromise—"I could buy those new shoes, but then I can't move out for another month." This is the process by which we learn a little about delayed gratification.

When you begin to invest in real estate, the tendency is to want to spend all of the profits as soon as they come in. But you must learn to resist that urge and protect your little fledgling pot of money.

There are a couple of amazing but simple strategies I use to combat the desire for instant gratification.

Strategy One: Pay Yourself First

When your paycheck comes in, what's the first thing you do? Pay your bills probably. That traditional way of thinking is great when you have financial abundance—and we are definitely working toward a point when you can get all your bills and debts coming from a separate account that you don't even need to look at. In the short term, however, you need to make sure you have some money to invest in yourself and your financial future.

More than likely, if you pay everything first, you'll be left with very little and feel that you don't have any money to invest—and definitely no money to enjoy. So pay *yourself* first.

I was mentoring John, a thirty-five-year-old guy who was pretty fed up when we met. He remembered having all these dreams as a young man, but somewhere along the line, all the dreams had fallen by the wayside. As he said, "life took over." Sound familiar? I told John that things needed to change for the sake of himself and his family. He wholeheartedly agreed, but when it came down to it, he insisted that he had no money to invest and no money to spend on learning investment strategies. It became pretty clear where we needed to start working. John earned $27,000 per year, or $2,250 per month. On payday, he usually transferred money to all of his bills.

Rent: $900

Utilities: $225

Car: $400

Credit: $350

Food: $200

Clothes/Entertainment: $175

Total: $2,250

At first glance, it appeared he had no money left to invest or move his life forward. He felt helpless. Helpless, that is, until we helped John to pay himself first. Without even changing his habits, John was able to consolidate his debt with a loan which saved $60 per month. He then took a look through his statements and found he was paying $20 for insurance—which he could get free with his bank account—and had a $27 subscription to a magazine he hadn't even received since moving.

That had already freed up $107 per month without him giving up anything! It's not an enormous amount of money, but the knowledge he could gain from spending those dollars on himself could transform that $100 into millions! The first thing John did was open a high-interest account in which he could stash the extra money. Each month, he transferred the $107 to himself before paying anything else.

The next thing John did was split that $107 into three distinct pots—investment, savings, and reward. I taught him to use 50:25:25 as rule of thumb. So he would invest $53.50 to get a better return on his money and ensure it was working hard for him, he would put $23.50 into a high-interest, low-risk savings account which is never to be touched and provides an extra level of security for himself and his family, and the final 25%—in this case, $23.50—was for John to do whatever he wanted. Maybe a computer game, a movie, a nice shirt. That money was for John to spend guilt-free, knowing that he had allocated to his future and was moving forward. Although not a large sum, this small reward helps keep the momentum going.

Sometimes things will come up which make some months a little tight, but if the money isn't there to spend, you find a way to survive—maybe a bill gets deferred or you only make the minimum payment—but if the money is there, it gets spent! It is absolutely crucial that you protect your investment pot and work towards your goal of financial freedom.

At the end of one year, John had transformed that $107 per month into $600 savings, ten books, two seminars, and a potential joint venture with a wealthy local businessman. That is the power of the compound effect. Slow and steady is fine, standing still is not. Do it now and do it regularly. Be consistent, and you will get the compound effect on your team.

If you ever doubt that you are moving forward and whether it is all worth it remember this—

The Chinese Bamboo tree takes four years to break the surface of the soil, but in just five weeks, it can grow to ninety feet. That is the power of persistence and the strength of the compound effect.

Baron de Rothschild was once asked to name the seventh wonder of the world. It is reported that he replied, "I cannot, but I can *tell you that the eighth wonder is the compound effect."*

Strategy Two: Take Control

If you ask most people what they spend their money on, they won't be able to tell you. There may be some vague stab in the dark about rent payments or car loans, but as for the nitty gritty of where it all goes, they will have no idea. The truth is if they are not in control of their personal finances when there is only a little bit of money to worry about, how are they going to manage and build their wealth as the pots become larger? Would you put someone in charge of your business if they couldn't tell you how their own bank account runs? Of course not.

We should all treat our personal finances as we would run a business. We need to become the financial directors of our home. It doesn't have to be complicated. As with every other part of my life, I look for systems and strategies to take the emotion and energy out of decision making. A great system is to have maybe five or six bank accounts. The first will be a cash account that everything you earn goes into and gets sorted and transferred from there. The second is an average interest secure savings account with poor immediate access, the third is an account with easy access for savings you might need to buy a new car or to return a deposit, the fourth account is used to accrue larger funds for investing, and the fifth is my fun Friday account.

Practically, this is what it looks like:

Purpose	% of Net Income	Purpose	Comments
Living Expenses	40-60%	This account is where all my income goes first. Bill and debt payments are debited from here, as are standing orders for the other pots of money.	Low interest, highly accessible account. Has perks like free insurance. Charity debits are set up to come from here.
Savings	5 -15%	This is for liquid savings. This money isn't to be touched or invested. It provides an extra layer of family security	Fairly low interest but accounts with delayed access (e.g. need to give 4 weeks' notice to access funds).
Unexpected Costs	1—5%	This account is for unexpected or low cost 'stuff'. For example, saving for annual car insurance, a new car, a replacement washing machine.	The account is quickly accessible with online access.

Fun Time Friday	5-15%	Fun/social/shopping. This is money to do with what I like. If the money is not spent within 31 days of it coming in, it gets sent to the investment pot.	Another cash account.
Investing	5-30%	Each lump allocated towards future investments is in here. When the project is ready, funds are transferred from here to builder/attorney (or whomever).	Moderate access, circa 2 weeks, tends to be low interest.
	Total must not exceed 100%		

You can see that the amounts can be amended to suit your situation. Whether you decide to have separate accounts for each is entirely up to you, but the more structured and systemized it is, the less likely we are to give in to a whim and, just as importantly, the less time in our day it takes up. If you have some debt, your figures might look something like this:

Living expenses 52%, Debt 23%, 5% Fun, Liquid Savings 5%, Unexpected Costs Savings 5%, and 10% Investing

By maintaining a disciplined approach and becoming your own financial director, you will soon reduce your debt. Your figures may then look more like this:

Living costs 45%, Debt 0%, Fun 10%, Liquid Savings 10%, Unexpected

Costs Savings 5% and Investments 30%

Where possible, try not to vary these amounts, just as a business wouldn't alter its course based on one good or bad month. Rather, refer to your wealth plan and schedule reviews every six months to monitor your progress. If your income has increased or your debt has decreased during this period, you may want to readjust some of the amounts to reflect this.

This is the difference between you living with wealth and abundance and you fearing scarcity and being afraid. Scarcity is a mind-set that is ingrained from a young age and comes from being repeatedly told not to want X because there is not enough money, or money doesn't grow on trees. When you live and make decisions from a place of scarcity, you cannot attract abundance. If your fist is closed to money flowing out, it also cannot flow in. You are captain of your ship and financial director of your home.

Strategy Three: We're All Creatures of Habit

"We are what we repeatedly do."

~ Aristotle

"Next year will be different." Year after year, people make endless resolutions about how their lives will be different. They'll earn more, lose weight, get great friends, and find a partner that they can be fully present with. However, when you ask them what they are doing to create that reality, ninety-nine percent can't tell you because they aren't doing anything. Therefore, nothing will change. They will go to the same bars they have been going to for the last ten years where they have never met the partner of their dreams, they will continue going to the job they hate that doesn't pay them enough, and they will continue to eat food with low nutritional value that's high in fat and sugar. Then twelve months will pass again, and the same thing will repeat itself.

If they would all stop for five minutes, take responsibility for their actions that have landed them where they are, and then consider which habits need to be changed on order to get the results they want, it could all be so very different.

You've heard it before, humans are creatures of habit. We like routine and we like to know what we should be doing at a particular time. If you need convincing of this, think about children. The most important thing you can do to improve a child's behavior and sleep patterns is give them a routine and stick to it. When you return to work after a break, how difficult is it to complete the tasks you would normally complete? Suddenly, it all becomes arduous and exhausting because you're out of the habit.

The quickest way to change your life and combat instant gratification is to form new habits. Habits like paying yourself first take the decision-making process out of day-to-day life and mean your decisions cannot be affected by your mood or whether or not you feel like doing it. Think about it, if you walk into the house after work, and your meal is already prepared and just needs heating up in the oven, even if you are completely exhausted, ninety-nine percent of the time you will have that for dinner. On the other hand, if you don't have a meal prepared, and you return from work exhausted, you are far more likely to grab a quick and unhealthy snack order takeout food.

Habits mean that you do things you are supposed to even when you're not in the mood. I often exercise in the morning, partly because that's the quietest time in my day before the phone starts ringing and partly because if it's the first thing I do when I get up, nothing can distract, delay, or interrupt me. I just have to get up, put my shoes on, and I'm already out of the house before I have time to consider whether or not I want to go out.

Use the free success schedule template in the members area to plan your week and make sure you are scheduling everything important—from family time to reading time to networking.

Everything that is non-optional should be scheduled, and then you must commit to it.

Action Steps:

Create your wealth map. Get a handle on all of your finances and make today the platform to catapult you into your future.

- Log in and download the tables, spreadsheets and resources to make setting up your financial plan quick and simple. We've done all the calculations so you just fill in the digits and figure out your instant financial status.
- Grab your success schedule – share your dreams with your family and prioritise your future

Chapter Three

Step Three: The Wealth Map - Where are you going?

Plan

As you begin your real estate investing career or make the commitment to up your game and play all out, your biggest challenge will be coping with overwhelm. At a time when you already feel like you have a full plate, to really claim your future and have the leveraged income and freedom you deserve in the short term, you need to push on.

The reality is, this can't be done on your own. None of us have the time, skills, energy, and interest to do everything it takes to build a real estate portfolio—profitably and quickly—by ourselves. I certainly didn't, and I definitely don't now.

I have a team. A great team that I'm incredibly proud to lead. All of them have different skill sets and passions. They have different drives and different motivating factors. When I learned the ingredients to the magic sauce that I'm about to share with you, it completely transformed everything I had been doing up until that point, and everything I have done since.

Planning always sounds boring and passive, so instead I call it Active Dreaming.

Hoping without a plan is just dreaming. So we need to *actively* plan and take the steps needed to move forward and make these dreams a reality.

Creating wealth, like most things in life, is simple. Does that mean it's not hard work? *Absolutely not!*

If your finances aren't in a great place at the beginning of your journey to creating wealth through real estate, the temptation is to bury your head in the sand and not look at your bank balance, credit cards, bills, insurance statements, overdue accounts, and the like. You are going to have to fight tooth and nail to get through that fear and face up to where you are now.

I suggest taking a pen right now, getting all your bank statements, and writing down each and every regular payment that goes out. Be sure to include your rent, insurances, credit cards, and any regular charges going to your credit cards, like your morning coffee. Really take your time and be thorough. This is your first step to achieving wealth. Once you've totalled it all, deduct that figure from your household income. And again, be brutal—you cannot base your budget on hopeful tips or occasional overtime. What income comes into your house each month? What figure are you left with? Is it a plus or a minus?

If it's a negative figure, don't panic. My figure was minus by several zeros, and I'm glad it was! Before you freak out and tell me I'm crazy, that don't I understand the pressure you're under, and clearly I have never been broke because I'm telling you that a minus figure was a good thing, let me explain.

The greatest enemy of action and success is comfort. With all the millionaires, billionaires, and super successful business owners I've had the pleasure of spending time with and now call friends, one trait is very apparent. They came from a place of pain and discomfort. There was something about their lives that was so uncomfortable that they had to change it, and they were determined and prepared to do anything it took to do so—whether it was pay for a mentor they thought they couldn't afford, travel to seminars when their friends thought they were nuts for going, work hours that could only be described as insane. They sacrificed their health, their time, their relationships, and their families. I'm not saying that's the best way, and it's certainly not the only way, but you get my point. If you're lying on a bed of nails, no matter how much your feet hurt, you're going to get up!

The Power of Real Estate Investing

It's like a superhero syndrome! Successful entrepreneurs are like superheroes. They were living a life that was unacceptable to them, they had a life-changing, decisive moment from which point nothing would ever be the same again (like Spiderman being bitten by a spider), and they transformed into creatures of strength and hope and courage. Learning how to manage the new life wasn't always easy, but they learned and then went on to help and uplift millions of people. That, my friend, is what I want for you.

Real estate, as we'll go on to show, is an incredible tool. There's nothing else like it, but it is still a tool that needs to be worked and used.

My moment happened a few months after becoming homeless. Up until those months, I had always gotten my friends, my sense of importance, and my love from people based on what I thought I had achieved by such a young age. No one in my family had ever been to college before, so the fact that I did that was incredible. I then continued on to be a successful physical therapist, traveling the world and working with national teams and premier league football teams. All of this made me feel invincible. I thought everything I touched was golden and nothing would go wrong.

So I started a healthcare center and, again, it went really well…until it didn't. In an incredibly short time, I lost my home, my sense of worth, my confidence. I didn't know what I had to offer to the world anymore, why anyone would want to know me. If you know my story, you'll know that I grew up in a poor environment where violence was prevalent. At twenty-one, I lost my best friend when she was murdered as a result of domestic violence. During my college and work years, I had thought that when I was successful, I would create fantastic centers to change the path of victims. I would wanted to create a charity foundation and do all these wonderful things that could maybe change at least a small part of the world. Then all of a sudden, there I was. Sleeping on an inflatable bed—that had a hole so kept deflating through the night—in a small room with no windows, no air. I had no shower facilities and no oven. In an instant, everything I thought I had known about the world was turned upside down. I thought I had nothing to offer.

A few months after this, I was sitting around, feeling hopeless, when it occurred to me that for all the excuses I had made to myself and everyone else about my situation, there were people out there doing it—creating wealth, being successful, and being happy. It occurred to me in that moment that if I gave up, I was not only letting myself down, but I was letting down my family and all those people around the world I had wanted to help. That was *my* superhero moment. That was the moment when everything changed for me and, as you know, within 12 months, I had a $2 million dollar real estate portfolio. Now I get to fund the building of schools in Africa, raise money for domestic violence shelters, employ out-of-work contractors, create jobs, and give back to local communities.

While those times were so painful and still bring tears to my eyes to think about, I want so much for you to have that moment. I want you to experience the event that changes everything for you and flips your brain upside down. So many people wait for something catastrophic to happen before changing their habits and their life. They have to fight from the bottom. In many cases, people wait until they have cancer to take care of their health. Or they wait until they lose someone to embrace loving fully. Or, like me, they wait until they are flat broke to work on creating wealth. Well, you don't have to hit rock bottom, and you don't need a cataclysmic event to force the issue. Let *this* be your turning point. You've already taken the step of reading this book. You're on the right path. Keep going.

So I say again that in many ways, a minus figure isn't a bad thing because you'll know the pain that comes from being worried about bills. You'll understand the pressure and the sleepless nights and the constant feelings of failure. If that is you, then I know that you are more likely to succeed than anyone else, and definitely more likely than those people you are jealous of wishing you had $100k to start off with. I promise you.

This doesn't mean that those who aren't struggling can't succeed. Of course not. It just means you have to be even more disciplined and even more focused because you need to create the urgency and the desire artificially. You cannot allow yourself to settle for mediocrity and average living. You are meant to be so much more than that, and if you continue, just making ends meet and having your annual family vacation and maybe upgrading your car every now and again, you will never live the life that is meant for you. You will never know the true freedom that comes from passive, recurring income. Or the unbelievable sense of space and freedom that occurs when you look at your day, week, or year and actively decide what you want to do. Or the feeling you get when you look out the window at everybody going about their day, doing the rush hour thing and barely surviving, while you are spending your morning reading or relaxing with a coffee, secure in the knowledge that you and your family are financially taken care of. That feeling is simply sensational.

When we start looking at where we are now, many people become defensive and retreat inside themselves, not wanting to know where they are. The truth is too scary. "I know I'm in debt, I know things aren't great. Surely that's enough. Do I really have to go there? Do I really have to face exactly how bad things are? Can't I just start earning more and let it figure itself out?" Sound familiar?

If you're feeling like this, you are not alone, there is a whole community waiting to help you, but you must take the first step and let us meet you halfway for two reasons:

1) Facing up to your situation and becoming an accountable financial director of your life is part of your journey to grow into the leader you will become. To attain the wealth and lifestyle you want, you need to learn how to lead your team and how to cope under pressure. When you are at the top of the tree, burying your head in the sand just isn't possible. They Need You.

When you begin to examine your accounts, you will notice a lot of patterns and habits. These are not only fascinating and enlightening, they also give you a more objective insight into your spending habits.

2) Simply put, if you know where you are going, but you don't know where you are, how are you going to get from here to there? Just imagine if I'm in town, and I called you and said, "Hey, can you direct me to the station, please?" "Sure thing, Kemi," you reply, "but where are you?" "Ah, well you see, I don't really wanna talk about that. It's a bit dark and a bit scary, and I'm not really happy about it, so can you just point me in the right direction?" You would 100% tell me it's impossible to give me directions until you know where I am, and this is no different. I can help you get there—if you want it and are willing to put the work in—but in order to support you, I need to know where you're coming from.

Besides that, when you achieve your goals, you get to celebrate and reward yourself. Pat yourself on the back for progressing through the journey. You can't do that if you don't know where you were or how far you've come. Rip off the Band-Aid.

Once you have your current income and expenditure figures, you know your starting point. The next obvious step to plan is where you want to go.

Keeping the Lights On

The first figure on your wealth map is your 'keep the lights on' figure. This is the amount of money per month that will keep your family with a roof over their head, food in their bellies, and warm. It doesn't include treats or extravagances. It's simply the day-to-day needs of your family. This is your first goal because even if you love your job and have no intention of quitting, whatever happens once you have that level of passive income per month from real estate, you are on the first rung of security. You are no longer reliant on a CEO or anyone else to keep you in a job. It might not be the dream lifestyle but at that point you are free, and you are safe. So work out your keep the lights on figure now:

Rent/ Mortgage:

Utilities/Living bills:

Car (Fuel and Insurance):

Food:

Debt Payments:

Total:

That's target number one. Your absolute minimum goal for the very near future needs to be that figure. When you reach that, you will walk a little taller, stand a little straighter, and you will pull your shoulders back and swagger down the street. Even if you hate your job at the moment, you might well find when you reach that figure, you actually don't hate it so much anymore. A funny thing about human nature is that we resent things we need to do, so as soon as you take that need away, all of sudden, you are in control and the hate melts away.

Don't misunderstand me. I'm not suggesting you quit just yet—we are going to leverage your job and income a bit more. But that is the figure you need to have coming in monthly, or a minimum of one year's total in an account, so should the worst happen, you can at least 'keep the lights on.'

Now for the exciting bit. What monthly income do you want when you imagine your dream lifestyle? The house by the beach, the Bentley, an infinity pool, two housecleaners, and a gardener? How much does that cost? If you don't know, check it out. Right now, go online and see how much your desired lifestyle costs. Check out the going rate for staff, maybe a PA or VA, the cost for a driver if that's what you want. Make a list of everything you want and the monthly cost for each.

Mortgage:

Insurances:

Cars:

Staff:

Holidays:

Total:

Great, that's now your *big* goal.

Right now, it doesn't matter how that's going to happen, and honestly it's not important. What matters is that you now know where you are going—and that you believe you will get there. I know you're thinking it's completely unrealistic and will never happen. I know you're battling with your life experiences thus far, and your common sense is screaming at you to be realistic and set smart goals. But the thing is, *smart goals suck!* People who tell you to set realistic goals are dream stealers. They are overly cautious and fearful people who will never make the total life shift that you want.

Here's why. You cannot discuss 'realistic' in the same breath as trying to attain true wealth and multimillion dollar real estate portfolios—because, of course, it's not realistic! It's not realistic to think that almost half of the world's wealth is now owned by just one percent of the population, but it's true. It's not realistic to think that the *Chicken Soup for the Soul* book series of over 250 titles has sold more than 110 million copies in the US and Canada alone after being rejected by 144 publishers. It's not realistic to think that I raised $1m in JV finance to buy real estate while I was homeless.

Realistic is that everyone works for fifty years earning just about enough to keep a roof over their heads, paying most of their earnings in taxes and then struggling on with whatever welfare and pensions payments you may be able to get your hands on until you die. Realistic is that heart attack rates triple between 6 am and 9 am Monday mornings when your body literally screams at you, *I don't want to do this anymore…YOU'RE KILLING ME!*

Reality sucks. If you want to do something extraordinary, if you want to live an extraordinary life, you need to set extraordinary goals. Brendon Burchard, the founder of Experts Academy and a *NY Times* bestselling author says, "Too many people have lost all grand ambitions for change and greatness by heeding the advice of the 'realists' and the standard bearers of the status quo, who tell us to set 'smart' goals." And boy, is he right!

This doesn't mean that you can't break your goals down into monthly, yearly, and five-year goals. It just gives you license to dream and to believe in your dreams.

While real estate is your business, *you* are the asset. If you hope to make money and attain wealth, you have to believe that you are worth it and you deserve it. The fact that you are reading this and you want to become an ethical, conscious real estate investor means you are worth it. You want to serve the world and add value while earning a great living.

Now let's get really strategic and detailed to show you how to grow your income and create wealth. The only way you get to a vacation or to a particular destination is by use of a really detailed plan. It's no different when you are trying to create wealth. Here we will delve into your business metrics and your key performance indicators. These will form the basis of your plan to wealth.

While you are building your real estate portfolio and getting to the keep the lights on figure, your first job is to maximize all the avenues of revenue and income in your life. This extra income will reduce your debts the fastest and increase your investment pot.

Strategic Wealth

Know Your Value and Get a Pay Raise

If you are employed, the fastest way to increase your income is to receive a pay raise. Yet research shows that only around thirty percent of people ever ask for one. Of those people who do, around fifty percent are granted a pay raise, so you could be throwing away an extra five to ten percent per year just because you haven't bothered to ask. What would a ten percent pay raise mean for your investing plans? Employers are under pressure to keep wages low and increase revenues, but there are some brilliantly strategic ways to show you deserve a raise.

The principles are same for everyone:

- Know What You Want — You need to know the going rate of someone in your position with your skills and experience. If you don't know what you want, you will never get it.
- Add Value — Give your boss the facts that will allow him or her to justify your increase. Ask yourself what financial benefits you have brought to the company, along with other non-financial successes such as how you helped with the efficient running of the department or any new ideas you have introduced that helped to improve productivity or efficiency.
- Plan — Explain what you hope to achieve, both with and for the company, in the next eighteen months. Demonstrate how you could further add value to your work and your team.

These strategies are so powerful. A friend had a job she had been doing for around seven years. She was earning an adequate salary, around $30,000 a year. One day, she noticed that another company was advertising. They had labeled the position differently, but it was essentially doing the same thing as she was currently—but they were paying $100,000 per year. Of course, all of her negative thoughts kicked in, the inner doubt. The what-ifs played over and over in her head. Ultimately, she decided to get some coaching on how to position herself better and show her value. A month or so later, she went for that job, and you know what? She got it! An extra $70,000 per year, right in her pocket. Just for assessing her metrics and knowing her worth. What are *you* really worth? Are you allowing yourself to be shortchanged?

Give Yourself a Pay Raise

If you are self-employed, increasing your income is even easier!

Let's imagine, for example, that you currently earn $3,000 a month by selling used computer parts. Presently it looks like this—100 parts per month X $30. But your goal is to earn 10% more, or $3,300.

To increase this you can either:

a) Work harder, longer hours and end up with less time to invest in order to sell more which looks like this:

Sell 110 X $30 = $3,300

Or

b) You can raise your prices by 50% to $45, selling less but earning more, which looks like this:

Sell 74 X $45 to earn $3,300

Obviously, the second option is definitely more preferable!

If you increase your prices like this, even if you lose twenty percent of your clients (which you won't), you are still earning more than you were before, and you have freed up more time to spend on building your real estate portfolio.

If you don't believe me, try it! When I was homeless and running the physical therapy clinic, I used this strategy, raising my prices by nearly double. I did lose about twenty-five percent of my clients but not only was I earning more, the clients I lost were frankly the ones who were a pain in the ass! They were the clients sensitive to price, not the value or great service I was offering them.

Brian Tracy, the self-development master, wrote the most incredible book called *Goals,* which completely transforms your view of the importance and power of setting goals. Amongst the pages of life-changing advice on how and why to set goals, he also provides many examples of people who have set 'unrealistic' income goals and completely nailed them! I won't ruin the stories for you, but I strongly suggest you go out and get yourself a copy.

Action Points

The future of your wealth depends on your wealth map. Where are you going? What does freedom look like for you?

- Set your Keep the lights on figure
- Set your BIG financial goals
- Download the 'How to get a pay rise' guide from your members area

www.freedompropertyacademy.com/book

Chapter Four

Step Four: Real Estate as Your Wealth Strategy

I love real estate. I love almost everything about it. One of my favorite things about real estate is that while in itself it is a wealth strategy, there numerous strategies within it that allow you to create either residual income, great big lumps of cash, or capital appreciation. It is important to note that it's possible to lose money in real estate if you don't treat it like a business, if you don't get educated, and if you don't have a support network and mentor. All of these things are necessary for you to really get the results you deserve and seek. This is a training book on the *business* of real estate, not on the individual strategies. I'm going to share the common investing strategies in brief to allow you to begin to decide which ones might be for you and how you can use the remaining principles of real estate mastery to create your million dollar portfolio.

Why You Should Be Investing in Real Estate

Real estate isn't a commodity, a fad, or a phase. People are always going to need somewhere to live. It's widely documented that the population is consistently increasing, and yet we are building on average 100,000 too few homes each year. Governmental advisors in cities around the world are screaming that there are not enough homes. The net result of this is that demand is being created for you. The population is going up, but the supply is not going up—therefore demand outstrips supply. This automatically makes available stock more valuable.

Since records began (real records, the doomsday records 1066-type statistics), real estate values on average have doubled every ten years, regardless of recessions, depressions, or any other contributing factors. So if you buy a property for $100,000 and do nothing to it, statically it is likely to be worth $200,000 in ten years.

I don't know of any other asset classes that do that and have done so consistently for so long.

Let's cover the generic foundations of real estate investing.

You Make Your Money When You Buy

At the moment, most people will be able to get a 75% loan-to-value mortgage from the bank. Lending criteria is a bit tighter than in the 2008 heyday, yes, but if you speak to a good broker, most people will be able to get a bank to give 75% of the price of a house. This leverage is incredible—and so undervalued! We'll talk a lot more about it later. If you ever doubt how fantastic real estate is, try going to a bank and telling them you've been offered a great investment opportunity and asking them to give you 75% of the cost. You will quickly be directed to the nearest exit! Banks are notoriously pessimistic about everything—stocks, bonds, businesses, the works. However, property is something they are not only positive about, but they will fund the majority of. That's because they know wise investment in a sustainable, reliable method that they have confidence in is a good thing. Stocks and bonds are simply pieces of paper with an assigned value. They have no tangible value in and of themselves. Real estate itself is tangible—land has value, and bricks and mortar have value. This is where the saying "safe as houses" comes from.

Now back to our $100,000 house. So to buy an asset worth $100,000, you only need $25,000 plus a little extra for costs and furniture. Let's say $30,000. If your property performs as expected, increasing in value at nine to ten percent per year, in ten years, the value of the property would be $200,000.

Here's the thing, though. Often, real estate will shoot up by twenty percent in one year and then not increase at all the next. The value is averaged. This is really important to note when making your investment decisions. If you buy for the short term and plan to sell soon, it is entirely possible that you won't make money because you are in the wrong place in the cycle. If you are buying with a plan to hold onto the property for twenty years, it doesn't matter where in the cycle you are because, over 10 years, the value averages out.

Going back to our house, over the course of ten years you have created equity of $100,000. Equity is the difference between the lending on the asset and/or the cash you put in and the value of it. So in this case, you've put in $25,000 and the bank has put in $75,000 for a total of $100,000. After ten years, the house is worth $200,000, so you have equity of $100,000. This means you have achieved a return on investment (ROI) of 300%, and that's before you even add in the rental income. This is far more than you would make in a bank savings or in most other legal investment schemes!

Now if you lower the amount of the deposit you put in, your ROI will shoot up even further! I'll show you how to do that later. Now you've bought your property worth $100,000 and have spent $25,000 on the deposit. You're sitting back, enjoying the capital growth in the property. However, at the moment, you are responsible for the monthly mortgage payment—let's say it's $312.50 pcm (per calendar month) based on an estimated interest rate of 5% pa. At the moment, you're paying that plus insurance and utilities, and this results in negative cash flow. This means the property is costing more than it's bringing in. All investments—whether you are planning on keeping them yourself or not—must cash flow positively, otherwise it has the opposite effect on your wealth!

Use the following calculation to figure out the cost of a mortgage payment:

Amount of lending X interest rate / 12 = Monthly mortgage payment on interest only

i.e. 75,000 X 0.05 / 12 = 312.50pcm

After you buy the house, the figures look like this:

Mortgage: $312.50

Insurance: $20

Utilities: $50

Total = Minus $382.50

The next step is to rent the property out—you can either do a single let, which is often to families and couples, or you can rent the property out as individual rooms. Let's assume you rent this property out to a family for $600pcm.

The figures then look like this:

Mortgage: $312.50

Insurance: $20

Utilities: $50

Rent: $600

Total = Profit $227.50

All of a sudden, the rent is paying the mortgage and all other costs, and you are left with a positive cash flow of around $225pcm.

Taking this into consideration, over the ten years that your property has doubled in value, it has also paid you $24,000 in total from monthly cash flow… Not bad, eh?

If you don't have the $25,000, put that to one side at the moment and don't get distracted by it—I'll show you later how you can and why you should buy properties without any of your own money. Prior to 2008 and the global economic crisis that has enveloped the world, real estate became fashionable, and everyone fancied having a go at it whether they had the faintest idea what they were doing or not. John Doe started watching *Make Money in 14 Seconds* and other ridiculous TV shows and thought it could be done without any strategy or plan. And for a while, John got away with it, but it didn't last.

John had seen that all you really had to do was buy a house, and by the time the deal had closed, the house would be worth more and you could sell it again. It was common for people like John pre-2008 to buy houses in the hopes that they appreciated in value, leaving them empty in the short term. This, however, is not how sophisticated investors do it. John was essentially gambling, and when the crash happened, he lost, and the casino won. It's hard to believe right now, while there is not much confidence in the market, that these days will come around again, and the Johns of the world will be doing the same thing all over again.

Millionaire real estate investors do not gamble. They make educated and strategic decisions based on evidence and experience.

Be greedy when others are fearful, and fearful when others are greedy. -Warren Buffet

There are three reasons to invest in property: 1) Cash flow, 2) Lumps of cash, 3) Equity.

Cash Flow Strategies

Cash flow is the difference between the bills and the rent that property brings in. It's what is left after you subtract the mortgage and other expenses from the rent.

Example:

Income	Expenses
$500pcm	$120pcm mortgage
	$50 letting agent
	$50 MOE*
	Total: $220
	Cash flow: $280

***MOE is Monthly Operating Expenses and includes insurance and other incidentals that come up.**

Every property you ever buy should produce cash flow, even if you have no interest in keeping it. When you are buying to sell, you are hoping that the property will sell fast enough for you to make a profit—and also hoping that no catastrophic or sudden world event occurs that will affect property prices in the short term. This is calculated guessing and can be very successful, but it's still guessing. If you follow the golden rule and make sure that the property cash flows positively, then even if the worst does happen and you are stuck with it, it's an inconvenience rather than a major financial problem.

Here are some fantastic cash flow strategies:

Cash Flow Strategy 1: Buy To Let

This is probably the most common cash flow investment strategy.

The premise is that you buy a property for say $100,000, put in a $25,000 deposit, and then rent the property out—usually to a family or a couple—for $600pcm, for example. There's one major hurdle to this strategy which you have probably picked up on. Do you have $25k to invest? If you do, how many $25k pots do you have available? How long will it take for you to save up another $25k? That's no way to grow your portfolio.

The key to this strategy: Buy at a discount. Professional investors always buy single let properties at a discount. Every one we have bought for ourselves and our investors has had a twenty-five percent discount!

There's a good reason for this. If you buy a property valued at $100,000 and pay $100,000 for it, you have to pay the $25,000 deposit and then save up another $25,000 before you can do it again. However, if you buy a house worth $100,000 for $75,000, something magical happens. A $75,000 purchase price for a house worth $100,000 using a 75% mortgage means paying in a deposit of $18,750 which initially saves you $7,000, and immediately gets you $25,000 equity. Sounds like a bargain to me, but it gets even better…

You then carry out a light refurbishment, which usually means redecorating, changing the carpets, and maybe replacing the kitchen cabinet doors (but not the carcass, top tip!).

After a few months, you can apply for a refinance, and that means either the same mortgage lender or another will come out and value the property for you. Because you bought it for below market value, basically at a discount, and you've done some cosmetic work to show you have added value, the lender will give you a current valuation of $100,000 because that's the market value, not the discounted price you paid! The lender will then give you a mortgage of up to 75% of the new valuation $100,000. In case you aren't there yet, 75% of the new valuation is $75,000. So the lender will release $75,000, of which $58,250 pays off the first mortgage, and $18,750 comes straight back to you!

If you consistently buy at twenty-five percent below market value, then you can build a massive portfolio on just one deposit! I promise you, buying at a twenty-five percent discount is entirely possible because we do it for our clients and ourselves each and every day. That is the bread and butter of our portfolio.

My first investment property was done in this way, and I've done the same week in and week out ever since. In the early days of investing, I only invested in the north of England because the properties were very cheap to buy, and the rents were very high in comparison, so when I desperately needed cash flow, they provided the biggest cash flow I could find. Also because I didn't have any money at the time and was trying to raise joint venture finance to buy them, my limiting beliefs were so strong that I didn't think it was possible for me to raise large sums, so I stuck to the little boxes.

One particular property we bought for about $26,000. We sourced this property through an estate agent we had made friends with. She called me to tell me a virtually derelict property was about to come to market and asked if I was interested. I immediately went to see it and put in an offer. It was supposed to go on the market for $40,000, I think, but I put in an offer for $26,000, partly because I thought why the hell not and partly because the property was fire-damaged so we weren't able to view the inside. Worst case scenario, it could have been a $50,000-$60,000 refurbishment. In hindsight, as an early project and given that we (my business partner Laura and I) had less than no background in building or refurbishment, that was probably slightly ambitious, and I wouldn't recommend it, but that event sums us up fairly well.

We had conducted area research and done due diligence, so we knew that the property could be worth around $120,000 in tiptop shape, but at present, it was worth about $40,000 due to the fire. Our offer was just under 75% of the current value, which fit our buying criteria. After some time, the offer was accepted, and we bought it with a JV partner.

For this property, the total figures looked like this in the end:

Purchase Price: $26,000

Refurbishment: $49,000

Buying Fees: $2,000

Bills during Refurb: $1,000

Total: $78,000

The refurbishment took three months, after which the property was rented out.

After six months, we had acquired a successful valuation of $120,000 from a lender and a 75% loan to value offer of $90,000.

The cash flow then looked like this:

Mortgage: $210pcm

Insurance: $30pcm

MOE: $100

Cash flow: $600pcm

Plus NET Profit $12,000—This is the difference between all of our costs and the mortgage pay-out ($90,000—$78,000= $12,000 cash in my pocket).

How many of those would you like? How many would it take to reach your keep the lights on figure?

Cash Flow Strategy 2: Shared Houses

Multi-lets are often called HMOs or room lets. Simply put, it means instead of renting out the whole house to one family unit, you rent out each room separately with shared communal facilities. This strategy massively turbocharges your cash flow.

Practically, it means that rather than renting out the whole house for $600 per family, you rent it per room for $420 and pay the utilities. Here are the figures:

Four rooms let at $420 = $1680

Mortgage: $250

Utilities: $300

MOE: $100

Cash flow: $1,030

So just employing a slightly different strategy massively increases the income from the same house by four times! Multi-lets do take a little more managing—they take on average one and a half times the amount of work as a usual family let, but for four times the income, it can be very rewarding!

Multi-Let Top Tips

Students Lets: Should be located within a ten-minute walk from the campus or site of study. Parking is not essential. A bed, desk, and wardrobe is sufficient for most student lets, however, if you are really trying to push the rentals up in some areas, you might add a hardwired flat screen TV. One oven, microwave, and washing machine is sufficient in the kitchen. No bills need to be included in the rent.

Blue Collar Worker Lets: Should be located within a ten-minute cycle ride from wherever your target market works—factories, docks, and so on. The same furniture would be included as above plus maybe some soft furnishings. Some bills are included—I include $15 per room per week for utilities, and anything above that gets billed back to them.

High End/Professional Lets: The prime location for these is a ten-minute walk from the center of industry, usually the city center. Include all bills and Internet. Professional tenants will happily pay top dollar, but they want convenience. Use higher-end furniture and stage the rooms using wall canvases and soft furnishings. Supply all crockery and cooking utensils along with two ovens. Workers tend to get home at the same time, and they don't appreciate having to wait until someone else finishes to cook their meals. Small steps like this will minimize your voids and make sure you have a great reputation for being a fantastic landlord.

Multi-Let Success Blueprint

This is a great strategy for generating high cash flow really quickly and one of the most popular strategies we teach for people getting into real estate and wanting quick results and fast cash. Although we knew this strategy was around when we started out, we didn't really consider it for years, as usually you don't get to benefit from the capital growth of the property. We quickly changed our mind!

The premise of the strategy is that you lease an entire property from a landlord as a single unit and rent out the rooms individually with their consent. I'll use one of our recent examples to illustrate how well this can work.

There was a property on a real estate portal that was on listed as both for sale and as a lease. It was listed at a price a bit too high for the area and, while it was in good condition, there were a few refurbishments needed to get it up to a standard lease. When our team went to see the property, it confirmed everything we thought—it would make a great multi-let. There were five bedrooms and two bathrooms, a new kitchen, and new carpet. To convert it to a multi-let, it needed fire doors fitted throughout, a fire system, a risk assessment, and a bit of decorative repair. All in all, about $4000 needed to be spent, and we knew it would rent for $2,800 per month as a multi-let.

It was marketed with a small agent that we had previously approached with some creative strategies. They weren't responsive to our approach, and the property was priced very unrealistically so there wasn't any point putting in an offer. We decided to just keep an eye on it and see how it went. After three months, the rent was reduced, after five months, it was reduced again, and after six months, they were advertising the first month free. So we knew the owner was motivated, and because of this, they were more likely to be open to something unusual.

We then checked the Land Registry database and downloaded the property details, the owner's name, and their residential address (although sometimes it only has the address of the property and not the owner's actual home address). It also shows the lending information on the property which can be really helpful for negotiating with homeowners.

In this instance, we found that the property was owned by someone who lived four hours away (unless you're a professional investor with teams and systems, managing real estate not near you can be a nightmare, even if it's with a leasing agent, so I knew she would be fed up) and it was unencumbered (professional investors leverage their assets to get maximum value, so this was another indication that she wasn't a professional and could probably use some help resolving the situation). I wrote her a handwritten letter that basically said I'm a local real estate owner and could offer her a guaranteed rent for a few years, with no maintenance or voids. I added my phone number at the bottom. Include only one point of contact on direct mail. If you start putting web addresses and email addresses, people often start browsing the web, get distracted, and don't take action. In my experience, one contact detail and call to action gets the best results. Within a couple of days, the woman called, and we had a great chat. Her husband, sadly, had passed away about eighteen months before, and she had received a large insurance payout.

She had been advised by a friend to buy property with the money to provide her with an income, and despite not driving or knowing anyone in the area, she decided to buy some houses in that region because of the yields. She then gave the properties to the cheapest agent she could find, and they had promptly done nothing with it! The agent had had the property for just short of a year by the time I spoke to her, and in that time there had been a couple of viewings but no takers. The lady had become thoroughly disillusioned and had put the property up to sell. The same agent had told her that if she were to add a new kitchen, it would sell quickly. He then proceeded to charge her $10,000 to supply and fit what was at best a $3,000 kitchen! She was now responsible for council tax and utilities on her properties, and she still didn't have any rent coming in.

We met at the property three days later after the woman had taken a five-hour bus journey to get to the house because she didn't drive. In this instance, the property needed $5,000 spending on it that she didn't have, but she needed some cash flow.

It's crucial to remember when using the MLSB that you don't own the property, so spending a lot of money on the refurbishment is out of the question. I will usually spend an absolute maximum of five to six months net rent on a refurbishment out my own money and as long as I have a five-year plus lease to make it worth our while. In general, we're spending approximately $2000 per property, and we have lots of creative ways of getting the owners to pay for any further work.

The property was set to rent at $600 per month, and we agreed with the woman that we would fund the refurbishment and pay her $250 per month until we had recouped the cost, which worked out to be around one year. After that, we paid a guaranteed $550 per month. She was ecstatic!

We told her we'd send the paperwork to her house to save her coming back, and she could mail the keys to us. To our complete amazement, she handed the keys over there and then and said we could sort out the paperwork at some point!

This is an example of win-win real estate investing. The owner is delighted—she has reliable monthly payments coming in with no tenants to worry about and no maintenance as, under the terms of the lease, we take care of all of that and there is nothing for her to worry about. Her property is being looked after by professionals, and she does not have to chase rent. We are delighted as we have a brilliantly cash-flowing property ($2,300 per month) for very minimal cost. Tenants are delighted because they have a high quality home with professional leasing agents.

The figures look like this:

- $4,000 Upfront Refurbishment
- $ 250 per month lease fee
- $300 per month Utilities and Bills
- Total Costs: $550 per month
- Rental Income: $3,033 per month
- CASHFLOW: $2,300 per month

She has since leased us three more properties under the same terms. So those four properties make us an annual income of over $147,000 per annum, and we have no mortgages and no credit checks. It took approximately two and a half weeks each to complete the refurbishments, and then the money started flowing in. After seeing the income those first few generated, we have since added this strategy to our business, and this week alone we have been offered fifty properties from a family of landlords.

Multi-Let Success Blueprint Tips

- You must use a management agreement or a commercial lease to give you control of the property. You must not use an AST. If you use an AST and then give your tenants an AST, you are subletting which will be in breach of the homeowner's mortgage.

- The whole point of this strategy is cash flow, so choose properties that don't require much work unless you want to convince the homeowner to splash out a few thousand dollars—which they won't deem as necessary or they would have done already. Remember you can't refinance, so don't tie up capital.

- Combining rent-to-rent with a lease option is a great strategy.

- You want a seven-year minimum agreement to make it worth your while and get a decent return on investment in terms of your time and money.

- Any leases of ten years or over are required to be registered with Land Registry in the UK. To avoid this, we use five-year leases with the option to extend in a further five years. If you structure it so that you have the option to extend, but the owner cannot terminate unless you are in breach of the terms, you have just as much security.

- As a general rule, the first three to four rooms of a multi-let property pay the bills, so be sure you can rent a minimum of five rooms to give yourself a nice profit.

- Reinvest the profits from the MLSB properties to buy cash-flowing assets that you own so you can benefit from the capital growth as well.

This really is an incredible strategy for giving you massive cash flow in a really short time for very little money. These properties were completed in less than ten weeks and came as a result of one letter. What would you do if you could increase your income this year by $147,000 in fewer than three months?

We have put together a free video training series on this strategy available for you to download now and get going with this strategy. If you put the action points into place, you could have your first investment property before the end of this book!

6 Essential Steps to Cash Flow Investments

1—Recycle your Cash

The quickest way to build your portfolio and continually increase your income is to recycle your money and leave as little 'in' the house as possible. If you are buying a house, then the offer price is the key to this.

There are a few key questions to ask yourself that will answer what your offer price will be:

- After all my refurbishment works are done, what will the house be worth to a lender? (Note that this is the price at which a lender will value it, not what the real estate agent will tell you) (A)
- How much will the refurbishment cost? (B)
- How much are the other buying costs? (C)
- What is the maximum loan percentage the lender with loan me? (D)

Offer price = (A x D) – B - C

Example: 19 Palm Street is a three-bedroom, two-bath house. In top condition, the house is worth $150,000. To achieve that value, you need to spend $20,000, and the legal, survey, and other costs add up to $5,000. You've been working with a broker and know you can get a 75% loan-to-value mortgage.

Filling in the equation (A x D) - B - C, you come up with ($150,000 x 75%) - $20,000 - $5,000 = $87,500. Therefore, $87,500 is your offer price.

If you buy the house at this price, you can do the refurbishing and put a tenant in, spending a total of $112,500, and then ask your lender to revalue the property. Based on its actual value of $150,000, they can release 75% of that, which is $112,500. Very cool. One pot of money can be recycled over and over, and it will build your portfolio for you.

2—Cash Flow: Does the House Wash Its Face?

On the face of it, a lot of properties have positive cash flow and are great investments, but when you look at it closely, they don't always cover themselves and can very quickly become a drain on your cash. When working out their income figures, amateur investors will take the rental income and deduct the mortgage, assuming everything else is profit. In reality, you have to consider the ten percent leasing fees (unless you manage it yourself), ten percent voids (unless you have advanced management systems—which usually take years to develop), ten percent maintenance (and this just covers little bits like leaking faucets and insurance). In the example below, it only takes one bad tenant that your insurance won't cover or a central heating breakdown for your entire annual profits to be completely wiped out. For a family let, a house needs to generate at least $250 per month for it to be worth investing in to ensure the property washes its face (looks after itself).

Rent		$650
Mortgage	$350	
Voids	$65	
Maintenance	$65	
Insurance	$30	
Total	$480 Expenses ($535 including leasing agent)	$170 Profit ($105 including leasing agent)

3 – Cash-on-Cash Return

There are some cases when you won't be able to recycle all of your money. For example, using the Multi-Let Success Blueprint (MLSB), you cannot refinance because you don't own the property, so leaving the set-up costs 'in the deal' is necessary. Sometimes a mortgage lender will undervalue your house—instead of saying it's worth $150,000, they will say it's only worth $145,000. How do you know if a deal is worth it? How much cash should you leave in?

Above rental yield profit, the other biggest guide to your investment is cash-on-cash return. Simply put, what return is the money you put in making?

Let's look at an example. We used the MLSB to get control of a property that was already a shared house with six bedrooms. It was owned by a tired landlord (there are a lot of these around!), and the property was looking a little jaded. It needed around $6,000 spent on it to bring it up to modern fire safety standards and the condition that we maintain under our rental brand, plus another $2,000 on white goods and furniture. In this instance, the landlord didn't have the money, and there was no way to get the deal done without paying for everything ourselves, at least upfront.

Cash-on-cash return is a great equation for taking the emotion and heat out of any situation. It is an objective figure that is comparable and very difficult to argue! In this case, the property would lease for $150 per room per week, or a total of $3900 per month. The monthly lease we needed to pay the owner had been agreed upon at $900, and the monthly bills would amount to around $400. This left $2600 net of costs per month. As a business, cash flow is king, and so it's vital before investing any money— especially an amount as substantial as $8000—to ascertain what the return of that cash is and how quickly it will come back to you. To work out cash-on-cash return, the equation is this:

ANNUAL CASH FLOW / CASH INVESTED X 100 = CASH ON CASH RETURN (COCR)

In this instance, we knew the annual net cash flow was $31,200 ($2,600 x 12), and the cash invested was $8,000. So we were able to do 31,200/ 8,000 = 390%

Although we were spending more than I would generally be happy to spend on a MLSB house, the cash-on-cash return was so fantastic that I was happy to spend it.

Our COC criteria is this:

A. Can my money be making a better return elsewhere in the same time period?

If the answer is no, then that's a big tick in the box. If I can make an equal or larger return, I revert back to time scales. I would take a 390% COCR in twelve months over a 500% return in eighteen months. Remember—money is fluid energy and goes to the most industrious. If the answer to the question is yes, it often comes down to point two and risk. In many cases, the larger the return, the higher the risk. MLSB is an enigma because although the COCR is enormous, the actual amounts of money put in are small which mitigates the risk substantially. Also, a landlord who is sick enough of the property to call you back is not going to want that house back unless you stop paying, so do a great job, and the house will be yours for as long as you want it.

B. Do I have enough control over the property to mitigate the risk?

If I don't own the property or have a very 'attorney heavy' contract in place, then I wouldn't dream of spending thousands and thousands of pounds as there is too great a risk. If, however, I've got a fed- up landlord with a MLSB, and it'll take a couple of thousand dollars to get a great return, then I'm in. It's worth the risk for me. Your ability to tolerate risk may well be different than mine. I know an investor who spent $100,000 dollars on a property they don't own with very few contracts in place, and for me, that risk is too high—however, that guy had a great relationship with the vendor, and he was happy to take the chance.

C. What will the money cost me?

There are two kinds of cost when you're looking at investments. The first is opportunity *cost. If you invest the $8,000 today, you won't have it to invest tomorrow. Obvious, yes, but often overlooked. Is the COCR return good enough so that if you are brought a good deal tomorrow, you won't be kicking yourself? The second cost is the* literal *cost of using the money. If you are doing a JV, you may be paying the investor monthly interest. If you use a credit card, the card will have an interest rate attached. Does the COCR cover the interest substantially? If something unexpected comes up, are you still getting the return you need to cover costs?*

4 - Control not Ownership

The paradigm in real estate is that the greater the cash flow, the lower the capital growth. In essence, the houses that have the best yield and pay you the most monthly are usually in areas that are less desirable where the values won't go up as quickly. As a result, owning them becomes purely about cash flow for at least ten years. Obviously, it's great to build a portfolio of cash-flowing properties, but do not confuse owning property with controlling property. Managing a property using the MLSB is controlling a property—you do not own it, but you do have legal control of it.

Owning a property with no mortgage or lending on it is ownership. Having a property with 75% lending against it is just controlling it. You don't own it even if your name is on the title. If you don't believe me, don't pay your mortgage for three months and then you'll see who owns it and who holds the keys!

As there is very little difference between ownership and control, don't get hung up on having to own everything! I made this mistake for several years, and it really held back our growth. I was obsessed with having my name on the title and owning everything. It wasn't until a mentor pointed out how ridiculous that was that the penny dropped. In these cash-flowing properties, you are in it for the monthly cash, so if you have a MLSB contract for five years, and then it expires and the owner doesn't want to renew, why do you care? You've had great cash flow for five years without the hassle of raising deposits or mortgages. BOOM!

If you have thirty properties, all on five-year leases that expire at the same time, and all you've done is buy fancy cars and material things you don't really need, then you could find yourself in a hole when all of these leases expire at once. The really exciting part happens when you have been really smart and strategic and have taken this cash flow and—instead of buying loads of cars (note that I said *loads* because I love nice cars as much as the next person), you have bought more assets.

In the example above, the property nets $31,000 per year. This becomes really powerful when you take that income and use it as a down payment for another property. That property then adds to your cash flow, and you can use that secondary cash flow to buy a nice car. The net result is that you end up with two houses, two cash flows for life, one asset, and a nice car owned outright. If you had milked the cow too soon, you would have killed your income, wouldn't have the second income from the property, and you wouldn't have the asset! That is the awesome power of the compound effect, and it is the fastest way to build true wealth.

5 - Money Making Boxes

Cash flow is usually killed when investors buy properties they like in areas they like or they do the refurbishment to a standard in which they would like. Here's the key: *No one cares what you think!*

Each residential town/city/village has 'good' areas and 'bad' areas. Even the worst house on the worst street in the worst city has tenants. Assuming the price is right and the property is safe, clean, and tidy, you will tenant it. (Common sense does apply here—an empty house in a town that was abandoned ten years ago probably won't). Tenants, like all of us, are comfortable with what they know. Just because you don't like an area doesn't mean it won't make a great investment spot. It just means you have to ensure you have the correct management strategies in place, like bringing a decent leasing agent in to manage the property. Remember, the better the area, (most likely) the lower the yield. Buy where the money stacks up is not necessarily in the area you like.

Similarly with refurbishments, do only the work necessary to reach the rent you're demanding. Each area and property type has a rent ceiling—putting in gold taps and Italian marble floors may increase the rent by a couple of dollars a month, but it's definitely not going to be enough to ensure you get a decent COCR from the added investment. If you're renting a penthouse in Manhattan, putting in the gold taps may not even be enough to reach minimum rent. The standard varies across the board.

We usually aim to go five to ten percent above the market rent in that area, and that can be accomplished by researching local rental properties, and bettering yours *slightly*. This usually includes a slightly nicer shower, a different type of flooring, and a fancy-looking kitchen tap. The reality is that these maybe cost us an extra

$500 on a refurbishment, but they will add $65 per month to the rent minimum, giving an extra $8,000 in income over ten years by which time it'll need a light refurbishment again (156% COCR in year one). In the meantime, it will drastically reduce our voids and enable us to find tenants quicker than anyone else on the block. Conversely, if we spent an extra $10,000, we would have to choose between taking a big hit on rental yield and COCR—and have the rent take years and years to repay the upgrades—or increasing rental fees to try and recoup the costs quicker. Putting rents ten percent plus above the ceiling for the area is generally very difficult. Tenants will not rent somewhere when they know the person next door is paying twenty percent less, even if the bath is lovely. If you're paying top dollar for your apartment, you want to live in an area everyone knows is expensive. No one wants to say "Oh, I live on that rundown block, but my place is lovely" if they can help it.

Learn to look at each rental unit as a box that makes money. Unless you are the target market for your unit, then your feelings on the décor, location, or flooring don't matter. No one cares what you think. Test the market, see what other units are renting for, and then decide. I have a house that we decorated as part of a market test. We put in patterned wallpaper of all kinds of funny hues, put in a colourful kitchen, and basically followed every fashion trend there was. It cost us a little bit more, but I thought we'd test it out. I hated it. Absolutely loathed and detested it—and planned on changing it as soon as it was vacant. In the few years since that was done, it has had two tenants. The first had to leave because they were moving out of the country but asked us to hold their details for when they came back, and the second signed up with thirty minutes of it being marketed without even seeing the inside. So did I change it? No, the market loves it. In fact, we did a few more in the area in the same way. A lesson to myself—I'm not the target market.

6 - Manage your Manager

The primary reason you have these assets is cash flow, so you have to guard and protect that cash flow with your life. In real estate, that means managing your manager. In my experience, people want to do a good job. They like praise, and they like feeling appreciated. However, people are either poorly trained and can't do the job, don't understand the assignment, or are motivated by something else entirely.

I hear time and again that my property manager is awful or my leasing agent doesn't understand what I mean, and that is probably completely true, but no one does anything about it. As a professional and strategic investor, your role is to read and motivate your manager better than anyone else. You must do whatever it takes to make sure they know what you want and what it takes to achieve it.

For example, many people don't understand the rules of eviction—and all states and countries you will have different rules. In your next conversation with your leasing agent, empathize with them and tell them you know how difficult you found it to understand all the rules. If they say, or you sense from them, that they find it difficult, let them know that you'll drop them an email with the main bullet points. Tell them you put it together as quick reference for yourself because you didn't have the time to trudge through loads of paper, so it might be useful for them. Then, a week or so later, give them a call and see how they found it and if they had any questions.

This is a fantastic way of passing any message across to your agent without them feeling defensive or embarrassed. By telling them you know how busy they are, you are empathizing and understanding, not complaining or criticizing. By offering a solution, you are becoming a part of their team, not their enemy, and are quickly becoming influential in their eyes. Just by talking to your managing agent, you can find out how they are feeling at work. Do they feel appreciated and valued? Do they feel they are paid sufficiently? We are all the same—we will work hardest for people who appreciate it, especially when we don't have financial struggles on our mind. If you can show you appreciate them, you will find that they begin prioritizing your properties over those of others. Before we had our current management team, we would send flowers, bottles of wine or a bottle of scotch (assuming this doesn't cause offense), holiday cards and birthday cards, or maybe a new handbag or nice set of cufflinks to the people who worked for us. We, in essence, became their friends.

Providing a financial reward can be tricky as it might be against the term of their employment, or even against their moral code, but if it's accepted, it can be an amazing way to be sure your property is treated as they would treat their own. We paid our agents a fee directly for every appropriate tenant that was found and signed up within forty-eight hours—this was on top of the usual management fee we paid to the agency. There are two steps to pulling this off without offending anyone or leaving yourself out of pocket.

> **A.** When you are alone with the agent, tell him that you have a friend who has a portfolio—you're not lying, your friend is me—who had to reduce the voids in her properties because they were leaking money. After looking at it, she discovered she needed voids to stay below forty-eight hours to make any money that month, but it was so much extra work to get the property filled that they offered to pay the agent an extra $100 directly each time they were able to pull it off. You then go on to say that the conversation prompted you to think about doing the same thing by analyzing your portfolio, and you found a similar situation. Ideally, you would like to stay with his agency, but at the moment the average void is eight days (or whatever it has been). You appreciate that he's done his best and that it is a lot of work, but if he did think he could get them filled in forty-eight hours, you would be happy to pass the extra $100 on to him because it made your insurance cheaper, reduced the chance of a break-in, and increased rent in the long term.

By phrasing it like this, you have given him the opportunity to say no because it doesn't work for him, for whatever reason, without making you or him uncomfortable. You have also given him the opportunity to say yes without making it about the money but by making it all about his providing an extra service.

> **B.** If you get a yes from the agent themselves, you then go back to the agent and renegotiate your terms with them. Something like this usually works: "While I am delighted with the majority of your services, the time it's taking to fill the properties is unfortunately too long and, as a result, between your management fee and the mortgage, all of my profit is being wiped out. I don't want to remove my properties from you, but another agent down the road has offered to conduct the tenant find for $150 cheaper, and I'm not in a financial position to turn that down. Are you able to match it?" They will almost always say no, but that's fine because your next move is this. "I understand you have your costs, and I definitely appreciate your value, but this is too much money for me. I can take all my properties to another agent and have to start over again, hoping they're good, and I guess then you lose all the commission. Or how about if you meet me halfway? You drop your fee by $75, I'll take the $75 hit, and we can work together to fill these voids quicker." This has gotten a yes every time I or one of my mentoring clients has used it.

Again, you were appreciative of their work, you did not criticize but rather advise them of your situation, and then you agreed to meet them halfway. What they don't realize is that you met them halfway from the starting position YOU set. Once this is agreed upon, you have a motivated agency wanting to keep you happy as you have subliminally threated to take your business away, a super-motivated agent that wants an extra $100—and it's only cost you $25 (the difference between the $100 you'll pay the agent and the $75 discount you negotiated). You could go for a bigger discount, but you run the risk of removing the motivation for the agency. You want your business to be profitable for them so they are motivated to keep you on their books. The extra $25 you'll get back in a heartbeat as they fill your properties six days faster than usual!

The other way to protect your cash flow is keeping an eye on the condition of property, so every six months ask for a copy of their inspection report, which they should have to ensure the tenants are maintaining it appropriately. You should also visit at least a sample of your properties once a year to check that the reports you have been given match what you or one of your team have seen.

Capital Growth/Gain Strategies

House Flipping

House flipping (also known as 'doing a flip') refers to buying a property with the intent to refurbish it and then sell it for a profit. The objective is to buy a property as cheaply as possible, add value to it, and then offload the property for a profit.

In an optimistic market, flipping is incredibly popular, and it seems like every one is doing it. When the market is rising, time is on your side. If you hold on to a property for six months, and the market in your area is increasing by fifteen percent per year, then you will automatically have made money (net of tax duties). The benefit to flipping during this time is that there is a lot of movement in the market, first time buyers are able to get favorable lending terms, families can afford to upsize, and the retired are getting great valuations so are selling up to move to a community or travel. In general, the market is buoyant, and everyone feels great. What does this mean for you? It means that you will probably be able to sell the property quickly and for pretty much asking price. The down side is that sourcing properties at the right price will be more difficult as the market becomes more saturated, and inexperienced people will be willing to pay more than you will as an experienced and strategic investor.

In a depressed market with fear and a little uncertainty, however, things are much quieter, and competition is greatly reduced. You can have your pick of properties at the price you want to pay. The amateur investors are too busy reading the papers and believing the world is coming crashing down to look past the noise at what is actually going on in the economy. *More millionaires are made during recession than at any other time!* Often, many people find themselves in financial distress, and by becoming an ethical, proactive problem solver, you can help home owners to find solutions and make money at the same time.

In a depressed market, the price you pay to acquire the property becomes increasingly important as you may have to choose between making a quick sale and getting the price you are looking for.

Doing a flip can seem overwhelming when you begin. There are a lot of aspects you need to pull together, but it actually doesn't vary very much from a buy-to-let investment. You still need to buy at the right price, you still need to complete an appropriate refurbishment, and you still need to get the end valuation.

There are five aspects to successfully flipping properties:

1. Acquisitions

Along with deal analysis, acquisitions can be the biggest drain on your time and resources. As a sophisticated investor, you will be offering less than the amateur on most properties. Therefore, in order to get an offer accepted, you will probably need to do more viewings on properties. No matter how hard you try or how excited you are about finding a project, after the first five or six properties, they will all start to merge into one and you won't be able to recall the finer details.

In most cases, you will put in an offer and it will be flat out rejected. The agent will continue marketing the property. Often, a few offers fall through on any one house, and so the vendor gets a little bit more agitated. They will then come back to you with a counteroffer a few thousand dollars higher—this has been as much as two years later for us. Unless you have a system for viewing properties and remembering these details without wasting more time and doing another viewing, it's impossible to know whether you can or want to increase your offer.

The easiest method to deal with this is to have a viewing sheet. A really simple spreadsheet that details each aspect of a property and leaves you some room to make notes. You can do this either on paper or using a tablet or smartphone while you're at the property. You can then take pictures and upload them all into a file on something like Google Docs or Dropbox. They can remain there until you get the call, and then you can refer to your file and make a decision within seven or eight minutes. Using this method also makes it easy to have one of your team—and if you don't have a team yet, you will before long—conduct the viewings. You can review the viewing sheets after the fact. We use this method and then make offers subject to approval. This means the agent can test the waters with an offer if he thinks the owner will go for it, or get close enough that he'll give us a call. Our acquisitions director will then visit the property, confirm all details, and confirm the offer. This is a great strategy for reducing the emotion and stress involved in the decision-making process.

The best deals by far are achieved when you can speak directly to vendors as this gives you an opportunity to connect with them and find out what they actually want, which is often very different from just an asking price. Going door to door is a very time-intensive activity to find motivated sellers who are looking for solutions and are open to being a little creative in order to find a win-win solution.

These are some of the guerrilla marketing methods we use to attract motivated sellers to us and reduce the time involved—bandit boards, postcards in shop windows, stickers, advertising on your car, leaflet drops, word of mouth, joint ventures, direct mail, lead generation websites…and the list goes on!

2. Deal Analysis

As soon as you start looking for deals and word gets around, you will find your inbox gets flooded with 'great deals' unless you fiercely protect your time and get a rigorous system in place for deal analysis. Otherwise, it will very, very quickly consume your days and evenings!

The costs that need to be include are:

- Purchase costs (including attorneys, surveys, and so on)
- Refurbishment costs (including planning, architects, utilities, permits)
- End value (Not optimistic, the fire sale price you could get if it had to be sold overnight)
- Sales fees (Including tax, agent fees, any commissions or profit shares)

Setting up a really simple deal analysis spreadsheet will enable you to just run the numbers and either eliminate an opportunity or put it on the pile for further investigation. This is what one of our spreadsheets looks like:

PURCHASE COST							
Purchase Price					0.00%	0.00	0
Solicitor cost	0		0.40%	0.00	20.00%	0.00	0
Stamp duty	0		5.00%	0.00	0.00%	0.00	0
Agency fees	0		2.00%	0.00	20.00%	0.00	0
Set-up BVI+Management							0
Building Insurance							0
Rights of Light agreement	0						0
106 Agreement + CIL	0						0
Solicitor Additional expense			0.00%	0.00	20.00%	0.00	0
Accounting Fees			0.00%	0.00	20.00%	0.00	0
Total Purchase Costs						0.00	**0**
FINANCE COST							
Funding(%)			75.00%				
Total Funding			75.00%				0
Arrangement fee	0		2.00%				0
Interest cost per 1month	0		11.00%				0
interest cost per 12 month	0		12				0
Bank Solicitor	0		0.30%	0.00	20.00%	0.00	0
Bank QS			0.00%	0.00	20.00%	0.00	0
Bank Surv.			0.42%	0.00	20.00%	0.00	0
Total Finance Costs							**0**
CONSTRUCTION COST	**sq**	**£ per sq**					**Total**
Basement GEA	0	0.00					0
Commercial GEA	0	0.00					0
Residential GEA							0
Refurbishment Total Cost				0.00	0.00%	0.00	0
Architect fees	0		3.00%	0.00	0.00%	0.00	0
Structural Engineer fees	0		1.00%	0.00	0.00%	0.00	0
QS fees	0		2.00%	0.00	0.00%	0.00	0
Project management				0.00	0.00%	0.00	0
Party wall Surv.	0		0.75%	0.00	0.00%	0.00	0
CDM				0.00	0.00%	0.00	0
Marketing				0.00	0.00%	0.00	0
NHBC Insurance				0.00	0.00%	0.00	0
M & E	0		1.00%	0.00	0.00%	0.00	0
Unexpected Costs	0		7.00%	0.00	0.00%	0.00	0
Total Construction Costs						0.00	**0**
TOTAL COSTS							*0*

Not all of the costs apply each time, but this is the first step to saving thousands of hours of time and being able to leverage other people's time and outsource this work.

Top Tip: As you are building up some experience with refurbishment prices, get some quotes from builders and contractors for a house you will probably not buy. Ask them for a detailed estimate. Using the average of at least three quotes, you are in a position to create a refurbishment costings sheet. This will detail everything from the cost of carpet per square foot to the cost of replacing a light pendant or a new boiler. Then your team can complete refurbishment costs based on the refurbishment costings sheet to gain a more accurate estimate that you can then use to create an offer price.

3. Financing deals

There is a popular myth floating around the real estate community, and it goes like this:

Kemi Egan

"Find the deal, and the money will come to the deal."

But the reality, in fact, is this:

"Build your network before you need."

Yes, it's absolutely true that if I found a spectacular deal and wanted to do JV to finance the project, I could arrange an investor very quickly—and I do regularly. However, it has taken a *long* time of building up a quality network of cash-ready investors that know, like, and trust me. In the beginning, while you have no track record and no relationships, it takes longer, and it's hard work. But it's absolutely possible. You know I did it in my first year while homeless, but it does take time, and being able to act quickly on great deals is difficult when you don't have a relationship with the lenders.

As soon as you start making any moves in real estate, begin networking—making connections, meeting people for coffee. Do the groundwork. Put together brochures of example deals and share them with those in your network. When this groundwork is done, you will then have a network you can call on, and only then will the money come to the deal.

Different types of financing options:

Type	Pro's	Con's
Mortgage	Cheap Money May get refurbishment costs as well No equity or profit share	They may have requirements about the type and condition of properties Takes time to arrange Lenders make their money from interest and don't like you using mortgages to flip
Bridging	Flexible No credit score needed Speak to a real person Great for nonstandard construction and quick completions	Expensive High arrangement fees Will want lots of security
Venture capitalists	Speak to real people Flexible terms Will share the risk Once you have a relationship, they will throw cash at you	Will tighten the screw if you don't deliver on time Will want equity share plus interest
Vendor financing	Cheap Flexible Terms to suit you	Takes a lot of patience explaining Attorneys can mess up plans Exit needs to be secure
Private finance	Cheap Speaking to a person Flexible Can get 100% funded Can be quick	Takes time to build up a relationship

These just give an insight into some of the financing options available. Your responsibility as the professional investor is to match the correct investment with the appropriate type of funding. Knowing which options you have available can put you in a great position when negotiating with agents. For example, if a nonstandard construction commercial property comes to the market, then I know that most amateur investors will run. This lowers competition and therefore makes my position stronger. I can then make a cash offer to complete within days because I can buy it myself, call up a high net worth investor, or perhaps get bridging finance and then swap the bridge out for a mortgage, which is cheaper after restorative works have been carried out.

4. Restoration/Refurbishment

Refurbishments are my favorite part of the process—well, maybe second favorite after cashing the checks! Refurbishments are one of the places you get to see the difference you are making in the world. As investors, we get to take something ugly and make it something beautiful and functional. We create homes. We have had great success and even joint-ventured with builders, and we have had some less than successful times. This is a summary of our learnings and how you can find the good guys.

I. Detailed Tenders

How you do anything is how you do everything.

When you put a job out for tender, be sure to include some specific requests such as *we have a number of jobs going on at the moment so please be sure to ref:XXXXX on the quote* or *please ensure your quote is received by 5 pm Tues Feb 2.* Contractors, like the rest of us, have strengths and weaknesses, but it's important for your business that attention to detail is one of their strengths. If they do not pay attention to simple requests at the start, they definitely won't once the job has started. These little hurdles just weed out a few that aren't right for you.

II. Schedule of Works

A schedule of works is basically a timeline of the job. It will usually be presented in a table with an itemized list of jobs on the vertical axis and time on the horizontal axis. Each job will then have an X or a tick next to the point in the timeline.

Asking for a schedule of works quickly assesses a contractor's experience level and the likelihood of him delivering on time and on budget. Initially, if you ask for a schedule, and they hesitate in any way, disregard that application. When you receive a schedule, look it over. Does it make sense? Even if you are not very experienced, there are a few key things you should look for:

- If windows need to be ordered, is that listed on the sheet? Windows—especially not standard sizes or frames—can have incredibly long lead times, so if they aren't pre-ordered, they will never be there in time.
- How many trades are planning on being in at the same time? Has the contractor listed electricians and plumbers in at the same time? It is possible for a simple job like a bathroom suite refit for multiple trades to be on site, but if a house needs new pipework throughout, having both trades in can wreak havoc.
- How long has he left for the plaster to dry? The contractor should have allotted at least two to three days, depending on your climate, for the plaster to dry. If not, the contractor is usually hoping you won't notice, using that time to catch up on other jobs that may be behind or they haven't thought to factor in.

I. No money up front. Ever. Staged payments always. Never under any circumstances pay a builder up front. Agree to a payment schedule that is determined upon stages of completion. For example, for a six week job, I would agree a 40% payment after three weeks upon completion of X works, 50% on completion of all works, and retain the final 10% for

30-45 days post completion for snag lists. A snag list is all those little bits and pieces that you don't notice until after a time. Retaining 10% means the contractor has incentive to come back and complete all agreed-upon items promptly.

II. Be sure you are given a quote not an estimate. In law, it has been successfully argued that an estimate is essentially a guess and can be interpreted as subject to change, whereas a quote is a fixed quotation and therefore should only be subject to change in extraneous circumstances.

III. Both parties sign the quote and the schedule of works.

IV. Check in or have someone check in every few days minimum. If things are not where they should be on the schedule, ask why not and what steps are being taken to catch up to the schedule. Remember, the compound effect works negatively as well, so if the builder is one day behind in week one, unless it is addressed, you can almost guarantee that they will be late by at least one day per week at the end of the job—and likely more. This can cause significant delays and subsequently delay you selling.

V. Have your contractor show evidence of their insurance. At the very least, it should be public liability insurance and builders insurance starting from a minimum of around $5 million, but potentially much higher depending on the size of the job.

5. Post Works Sale

This is the really fun bit—and definitely the most nerve-wracking for your first few projects while you wait to see the benefits of your hard work. You should know within two to five percent what the property will be worth and the sale price before a single screw is drilled, so in many ways this is out of your hands, but there are, of course, a few super strategic ways to guarantee you get the biggest appraisal and sale price.

I. Stage the Property

Not everyone has a great eye for interior design, and so we have difficulty imagining how a space will look with furniture. By staging the property and putting in the best furniture for the size and shape of each room, you can add five percent to the perceived value of the property, thereby increasing the sale price. Likely, the new buyers will also want the furniture you have included because it will be perfectly chosen, so you make extra profit by selling the furniture as well. If you don't have an eye for interior design, there are some fantastic people around that do this professionally for really, *really* reasonable fees.

II. Pay the Agent

Most people are trying to screw the agent down and get their fee as low as possible, but do the opposite. If the agent is going to get 1.5% for selling one person's property and 2.25% for selling yours, whose do you think they will put more effort into? Yours. That's exactly what you want—the agent motivated to sell your unit for maximum profit. Figure out some kind of staged payment that rewards the agent for selling at the best price and for selling quickly. We usually do something like an extra 0.5 percent if it is sold within three weeks, and they get 0.25% of anything above the asking price they achieve. The results would amaze you!

III. Agent Exclusivity

Give the agent exclusivity to sell the property for a maximum of two months, but after that, be sure that you have the right to take it to other realtors. A lot of buying and selling of real estate is psychological, so if buyers see a house lingering on the market too long—even if it's a great property in great condition—they will assume something is wrong before they even look at it. You want your property shifted as quickly as possible. Time really is money!

Purchase Options

Purchase options are an advanced strategy that has been used for decades in commercial property, and only for the last five to ten years in residential property. A purchase option is exactly as it sounds. It is a contract that gives you the option to purchase a piece of real estate.

Commonly in commercial real estate, a developer would find a piece of land or a building that they wanted to build on or convert into apartments. Before they began using these contracts, the developer had two choices. A) Buy the real estate and hope they could get planning, and if not, hope they could sell it and recoup some of their losses. Or B) Apply for planning consent prior to owning the real estate and hope the owner didn't then decide to sell it out from under them or increase the agreed-upon price once planning was granted. Both of these choices are high risk and not a great way to run a profitable, scalable business. It was this situation, as with all innovation, that forced developers to be creative and get to work with attorneys trying to find a solution. The most effective resolution proved to be using a purchase option, and they have been commonly used since.

These options can be fairly simply contracts with a few crucial covenants:

- Mr X has the right but not the obligation to purchase 123 High Street for $X.
- The option lasts for X number of years.
- During such time he is responsible for the upkeep, maintenance, and mortgage of the real estate.

These covenants are critically important to protect both the buyer and the seller. Initially, the buyer has the right to buy the property for a set price during a specific time period. This ensures that whether planning is granted or gold or oil is found in that land, the buyer has the right to buy it for the pre-agreed price. The buyer can plan the rest of the project knowing that the purchase price is set and cannot be altered. The buyer also has protection as they have the right but not an obligation to buy the real estate. In essence, if they don't want to, they don't have to buy it. If planning isn't granted, they can walk away from the deal. A very safe position for the buyer.

On the other side, for the duration of the contract, unless they have inserted a break clause, the seller knows that the maintenance, mortgage, and upkeep is being taken care of. If the vendor is in financial distress and at risk of missing mortgage payments and subsequently being foreclosed upon, then this is a fantastic solution.

Once the investor is ready—as long as he is still within the allotted time frame—he can then purchase the property. The exciting thing with option contracts is that they can be assignable, that is to say they can be transferred to someone else. We have used this strategy with vendors in negative equity. Let's look at a recent example:

Mrs James owned a house that she bought in November 2007 for $250,000 with a 90% interest only mortgage. As we know over the next few years the market nose-dived and in her area hasn't fully recovered yet. In the years since Mr & Mrs James have had three children and are now very cramped in the house. They are desperate to move somewhere bigger so the children have their own room but as the mortgage was interest only they still owe $220,500 and the house is only valued at $205,0000.

Traditionally, Mr. and Mrs. James would only have had a couple of options—

- Stick it out until the market rises and then hope they can sell to pay off the lending
- Save up even more money to repay the loan out of their pocket but then have no money to use as a deposit for their next home
- Become accidental landlords and rent the property while renting a new home for themselves somewhere else

As you can see, none of these choices are very appealing to a young family that doesn't have $20, 000 to hand to a bank or the interest or time to manage tenants or a leasing agent. Fortunately, our team did some research and came up with an option contract that was really a fantastic solution for everyone. We agreed on the following:

- 10-year option to purchase contract
- Purchase price of $230,000 for the first five years
- If we have not bought the property within five years, we increase the sale price by one percent per year for the remaining five years or until bought.
- For the duration of the option agreement, we pay Mr. and Mrs. James double the mortgage payments.

So in this instance, the family will walk away with $9.5K minimum in their pocket after five years, whereas they would get nothing now. For the duration of the contract, they will earn $325 profit per month with no stress and no managing of tenants, which is worth over $19,000 for the term. If we assume we buy the property after five years, as is the plan, they will have gained $30,000.

We benefit because we can rent the property out for $1100 per month and earn $400 per month profit. Also, our enhanced due diligence process and risk appraisal suggests that after five years, the property will be worth $245,000, so we will receive a discount of $15,000on our purchase. That really is a win-win scenario.

I receive a lot of questions about option agreements and their status, so I'll address the top four now.

Q: Are they legal?

A: Each state and country has their own laws, but I am unaware of any region in which they are illegal. At its root, an option is simply a contract to buy at a later date, similar to an auction. You might put in a bid on a property over the phone, and the agreement is that if by 5 pm a higher offer hasn't been received, then you will buy it. By using a purchase option you are still agreeing to a sale price but simply extending the period over which the purchase takes place.

Q: How do you explain it to owners?

A: I ask the owners what they would like to happen. They usually answer with something like, "I would like you to buy the house for $X," to which I reply, "Okay, I can do that, but not for X number of years. In order to fit into my portfolio, it has to fill certain parameters, and that price is a little higher than I can pay right now." This explains to the owners that you aren't arguing with the valuation, and you respect their request, but that it doesn't work for you right now. It subsequently shows that you have a solution, and this keeps them feeling happy and moves them forward. I tell them that all of the contracts will be drawn up by attorneys, just like a normal sale, and they can move on as they were going to. Just keep it nice and simple and tell the truth. If you are truly coming from a place of wanting to help and finding a win-win solution, you should have no problem explaining it to them in a language they understand and can relate to.

Q: What if the person you are buying it from dies?

A: In most countries, contracts outlive people, so the agreement will become part of the estate and will be honoured by the executor of the last will and testament.

Q: My usual attorney hasn't heard of purchase options. What should I do?

A: Find another attorney! Your team needs a great lawyer for you to carry out sophisticated and advanced transactions that benefit everyone. If your current one can't help you to do that, I suggest finding another one.

Planning Gains

Planning gains are a brilliant strategy, especially when tied in with an option contract.

A planning gain is taking a piece of land or real estate and adding value by way of getting planning permission for a usually residential development. For example, a piece of land might be worth $50,000 as it is, however, once that land has planning permission to build 10 houses on it that are worth $200,000 each and the value of the land shoots up.

As investors, we are always on the lookout for something we can add value to and leave our mark in the world. Again, there are times when buying some real estate is too risky, but you can take control of the land with an option contract and apply for planning permission. Once you have planning permission, you have three main choices:

1. Buy it yourself and sell it on to a developer to build on.

2. Buy it yourself and build on it yourself.

3. Let someone else buy the contract from you so they can buy the land/building.

My favourite is choice three. That contract could easily be sold for $50,000 without you lifting a finger. A fantastic return on investment, given you will only have spent the cost of getting planning, and you get to roll on to the next investment with an extra lump of cash.

Title Splits

Title splitting is a very simple but advanced strategy that is almost never used! If you can get your head around it, you will spot hundreds of opportunities to use this strategy within your own town.

A ten-pack of chocolate bars might be $3 whereas buying the bars individually would cost 50 cents each. So if you buy a pack for $3 and sell the ten bars individually you will make $2 profit. The principle is that you buy wholesale and sell retail. If you go on a realtor's website, you will see small or even very big apartment units. Let's say the apartments are worth $90,000 each and there are 10 in a block. It's common for the block to be available for $700,000. So you are instantly getting a discount of $200K, plus owning the ground the block is built on. The reason for this is simple. There is less competition at the higher end of the market than there is at the lower end, so there are less people with $700K to spend than there are with $200K. As a result, there is more supply of these blocks than there is demand, and the value is affected. As sophisticated investors, you are going to learn all about joint ventures, so you will have more than enough money to buy any property you want.

When you purchase this property (or sign an option contract), you then ask your attorney or conveyancer to create separate titles for each of the apartments. You can then sell each of the apartments for the full $90,000. We would use this strategy to sell eight of the block and recoup all of our initial investment—and then keep two apartments for free.

Look at the figures:

Purchase: $700,000 and Fees: $10,000 = $710,000

Sell eight units at $90,000 = $720,000 plus two units remaining (value $180,000) and ownership of the block

Choose Your Strategy

Whichever strategy you choose as your favourite, this won't be your *only* strategy. In fact, we know that most millionaires have at least seven different income sources!

The reality is whether it's flipping or buy-to-let, unless you have prior knowledge on intelligent investing using that strategy (and living in a property doesn't mean you know how to invest in it), this will be a long term journey with a lot of success and a few slipups. There is no such thing as 'get rich quick'. There are, however, intelligent, educated, strategic, and ethical wealth creation strategies that can transform your life quickly. So you're going to need to educate yourself and immerse yourself in books, podcasts, seminars, and whatever it takes to step into the world as a an educated investor.

If you're anything like me, your chosen strategy will consume you. For a while, it will be everything you think about, everything you read about, and most of what you talk about! That's okay. This is your ticket out of 'averagedom' and 'reality'. Let it wash over you, and take it all in.

When you've chosen the strategy, use your goal metrics again. Let's take a second to run through some examples:

If you want $5,000 per month from real estate, what does that equate to? Have a quick look online at rentals in your area. What do they go for? It might be ten family apartments, or accommodation shared by five students. It doesn't need to take long—you're just training your mind to think this way and starting to allow the law of attraction to kick in. It doesn't end there, though. Remember, the law of attraction relies on you taking action! You now know what income you have, and you know where you would like to be. Combine this with knowing roughly what your asset requirements are (e.g. ten family apartments), and you're nearly there.

Time Is Your Biggest Asset

The third metric you need to know about is your time. What time do you have available, and more importantly, why? The most common answer I usually get is, "Kemi, I work full time, and I have kids. I don't have any time." Bad news, no sympathy here. Do you have a TV? Do you drink alcohol? What do you do with your time once the kids are in bed? I ask this not because I'm judging, but rather because we need to get serious. The time for excuses has passed. You can have excuses or you can have wealth, but you can't have both. Which do you want?

This is what a typical week looks like for most people:

- Work: 45 hours
- Commute: 6 hours
- Chores: 10 hours
- Sleep: 50 hours
- Kids' stuff: 14 hours
- TV/Movies/ Computer Games: 37 hours

And what do you know? They have no time! Scary, isn't it? What would happen if people changed their week to look like this:

Work: 45 hours

Commute: 6 hours

Chores: 10 hours

Sleep: 50 hours

Kids' stuff: 14 hours

Exercise: 2 hours

TV/Movies/Computer Games: 10 hours

Time to invest in yourself: ***31 hours!!!!!!!***

The world would be a different place if everyone invested thirty-one hours into themselves, their wealth, and their charities each week! What would your life look like? That still gives you on and a half hours per day to watch TV if you insist. And by the way, if you watch anywhere close to that, you're missing out on life!

We all have the same amount of time per week. Whether you waste that time or invest it is up to you. Work out your current time metrics. Where is there room for improvement? What are you spending a lot on that doesn't need it? This is personal. It's only for you to see, but be honest because time is one of your biggest assets. When you start building your wealth, the time you have to put into it will go a long way toward determining how quickly you get there.

Action Steps:

Start to get excited! Use the Freedom Property Academy roadmap to start to choose the best strategy for your situation and your area. Using the resources in the members area start to do some example deals. Log on to an online portal and use the documents to practice due diligence, checking the numbers and becoming a real estate investor.

There are some extra training videos on the strategies as well.

Chapter Five

Step Five: And Now to Turbo Charge

Focus

For most of us, wealth is a brand new world. It's full of exciting opportunities and things we didn't even know existed. The fog has been lifted, and suddenly we see business opportunities, flips, options, title splits, shared houses, and multi-let success blueprint opportunities everywhere we look. We finally realize that the world is full of opportunity, income streams, and possibilities. Of all these opportunities, the perfect strategy for one person might not be the right one for you. If you're anything like me, you will actually want to try them all. When I got a taste for the wealth that real estate gave me, I not only realized how much more fun life was, but what a difference I could make in the lives of others around me. The possibility was overwhelming. I wanted it all, and I wanted it now.

Which path to take is a very personal choice. There is no right answer—you just have to make a choice. The temptation is to develop magpie syndrome, becoming attracted to anything that sparkles and flitting between loads of different real estate strategies, trying them all but committing to none. You must resist this temptation with all your might. Wealth-building can happen fast—really fast—but still not as fast you'd probably like. It's important to remember that you are in it for the long game. You are doing this to make a difference in the world, to create massive wealth, and to leave a legacy. This requires a focus and a commitment that not many people have. You are taking a step up from being an individual and thinking only about your own needs to thinking about how you can make the most difference in the world. Making a difference requires us to be great—the best we can. It requires that we deliver massive value and serve the world. *One Step At A Time.*

Successful entrepreneurs work hard at maintaining focus, deciding on one plan and sticking with it. On your quest to create wealth, there are many different vehicles. The options listed above are all valid choices, and they all come with their own opportunities and challenges. The wealthy understand that simple consistent action directed in one focused direction will outperform random and spontaneous acts across a variety of activities.

Before you take any steps, research all the opportunities available to you and decide—based on knowledge and education—which one you want to pursue. You can create success with any of the strategies I've outlined for you, but the key is to become an expert in the subject and never give up or be distracted by the next shiny penny to come along.

Up your game

We are all guilty of this.

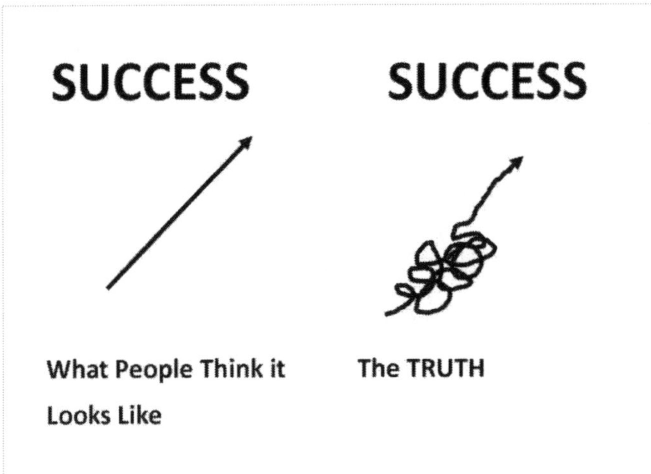

We read the books and go to the seminars and believe that it will all be straightforward with no hiccups. As a result, when we hit a hurdle, it shakes our belief systems, and we start to question everything we thought we knew, along with our decision to pursue wealth. The doubts start to kick in, and we revert back to what we know, usually learned negative habits that don't serve us well. So let me try and combat that now. There *will* be hurdles, and you *will* have bad days. There are going to be challenges you couldn't have even imagined and, yes, you might 'fail'. However, if you stand up, straighten up, and continue onward, victory will be yours. I don't share this with you to frighten you or dissuade you from the challenge, but rather to help you identify the stages of the journey upon which you are embarking.

Right now, you are playing little league. You're having fun with your friends but not playing full-out and getting the results you want. What would happen if I dropped you in the middle of a pro ball game with no warning about what was to come? It would get ugly very quickly! Conversely, what would happen if I warned you that stepping up your game meant the ball came faster and the opposing guys were a step faster, and then I let you watch a game or two before trying it? Do you think you would be better prepared? Absolutely. It might still be scary, and you might make a couple of mistakes, but you would know what is to come, and you would regroup quickly.

In life, as in sports, when the pressure is on, our behavior pattern is to do what we've always done. The only way to overcome this is to engage in learning new tools and coping mechanisms while the pressure is *off*. Previously, when I was feeling that pressure, I was prone to decide it was quicker and easier to do things myself than to delegate to my team—who would have truly done a fantastic job. This approach only compounded the situation because then I was taking on extra work I didn't need, spending ages completing it because I wasn't good at it, and then producing a lesser quality end product. Ridiculous! To try to overcome this habit, I set myself a target of outsourcing or delegating absolutely everything humanly possible for a few months in order to create a *new* habit—delegating over doing.

It's vital to understand your tendencies. When entrepreneurs are new to any strategy, they are nervous, anticipating and waiting for the results of their hard work to start coming in. When the financial rewards don't arrive as fast as they'd hoped, panic starts creeping in, and those doubts and inner voices reappear. Most often, those pesky voices will tell you to revert to what you know—giving up, quitting. You have to fight the fear and commit to the journey. If you do this, you will become an expert faster and earn the big bucks.

Take Roger Federer, for instance. He didn't dabble in a bit of tennis, a bit of soccer, and a bit of basketball. He committed to one path. Sure there were hurdles and challenges, but soon the compound effect was on his side, and he was the best tennis player in the world. What happened next? He added income streams to his revenue to reduce risk. He gained endorsements (hands-free income), investments (leveraged income), and built his brand (business), so while he plays tennis (earned income), he is also building a financial legacy.

The same is possible for you, and it's called the 80:20 set and forget technique.

80:20 Set and Forget

In wealth creation, as in all other areas of life, Pareto's principle is king. Pareto was a mathematician who first coined the 80/20 principle. That principle says that in any area of your life, 80% of the results will come from 20% of the effort. This has been shown to be true in so many areas. I strongly recommend you read Richard Koch's *The 80/20 Principle.*

To break it down further, the principle says that 80% of your profits will come from 20% of your clients, and 80% of your hassles will also come from 20% of the people in your life. It's an incredibly powerful principle. Imagine for a second that 80% of your income comes from 20% of your activities. So if you work Monday to Friday and earn $20,000, the work you do only on

Mondays creates $16,000 income. Knowing that, could you possibly readdress how you spend the other four days and increase the value of those activities?

When you decide which real estate strategy you will use to create your wealth, remember that 80% of your results will come from 20% of your activities. As Abraham Lincoln said, "If I had five hours to chop down a tree, I would spend the first four sharpening my axe." Your first job in those early days is to sharpen your axe—to gain as much knowledge as you can, to surround yourself with as many experts and mentors as possible, and to become as knowledgeable as possible as quickly as possible.

Once you've got the basic knowledge, it's time to start taking strategic, consistent action. Wealth will accrue quickly, albeit not as quickly as you would probably like! There is no such thing as getting rich quick. You are in this to create long-term, sustainable, ethical wealth and the foundations of an amazing legacy. Legacies are not made from chasing the elusive shiny penny but from having the discipline and focus for long-term strategies. Once your strategy is decided, commit yourself wholeheartedly to it for 80% of your time. Don't waiver on this. Take your time to learn the strategy, and then test it. Test different procedures, different avenues, tweak your marketing and systems. Maximize the revenue, and then test it again. Once you have gotten it down in a system that is profitable, ethical, and scalable, begin to delegate and outsource everything. Train your team, outsource, and then train some more.

Your first income stream is set up.

During that period, you were focusing 80% of your time on it. Why 80%? Because the other 20% of the time was spent researching and taking the first steps to begin your next income stream. You may have one or two ideas that you are considering pursuing. Spend the other 20% of your time testing the market, doing research, getting some more education, reading up on things, and then beginning a new venture.

Real estate is a fantastic vehicle for creating wealth through multiple income streams because it gives you have the opportunity to leverage the skill, knowledge base, and resources you already have built up to reduce the learning curve and time to get results. If your first income stream is a portfolio of rental properties, and you have a team managing them, it is simple to expand that to managing other people's properties and owning a leasing agent. Once you have set that up and extracted yourself from the day-to-day running, you rinse and repeat. A great extension to your portfolio and leasing agency could then be adding an income stream by helping cash-rich, time-poor investors to build a hands-free portfolio using the team you already have in place. These slight deviations use all the tools and materials you already have at your disposal, but they gently move you into having an income stream in another sector.

This is how we structure our business development, and it works well for our clients and for us. Eighty percent of our time, we focus on one income stream/business. We use this time to maximize the profit potential in that revenue stream. Once we have tried and tested different things and know what works, we create systems based on that. These systems include everything—from the day-to-day running of the business, telephone scripts, and customer query responses to business growth processes. We then produce guides, staff handbooks, and videos to allow our team to continue to do great work without my personal day-to-day input. And that is called 'Set'—you have set the business up. During this time, the other 20% of my time is spent researching a maximum of two other opportunities or income streams.

Once the first business is set up, and the systems are working and have been tested, you can then 'forget' it. The second business moves in to take center stage and takes up 80% of the time with a third business becoming the next 20%. Following this system will allow you to quickly and efficiently add income streams and create wealth and security for your family while reducing the risk of becoming overwhelmed and avoiding the confusion that often initiates the magpie syndrome.

Front Load your Mistakes

When you focus on one strategy, you are learning as you go. You will make mistakes—and hopefully a lot of them. In those early days, if you are following the system, you will be testing as you go along, and you will have very little to lose, so it's best to make all the mistakes you can as quickly as you can and learn from them. When you are onto bigger projects and have more riding on them, that is when you'll want to limit your mistakes. You will still make some mistakes, of course, but because you remained focused on learning one strategy and frontloaded all of your mistakes, they won't be as costly.

Time and again, people initiate a new strategy and start making mistakes. The results don't come as quickly as they hoped (mainly because deep down they are hoping for a get rich quick strategy) and then just as they get through that section and start moving forward, slowly gaining momentum, they quit and start something new. They then repeat this with the next strategy, frontload all their mistakes, and move on just before they start seeing results. These are the people you will hear declaring that they've tried everything and nothing works. Or they tried real estate, but it's impossible to make money from it. Frontloaded mistakes are your reward for focus and commitment. As you gain in experience, your mistakes will become happy accidents because experience will have honed your instincts, and your gut will begin telling you which step to take next. Fail Forward Fast.

Multiple Streams of Income

Multiple streams of income are absolutely crucial for your wealth. Relying on just one income stream leaves you vulnerable to changes in the market and small changes in legislation. Technology or governmental changes can leave your income seriously depleted.

Over the last few years, we have seen the drastic changes that have occurred in the world. It would previously have been unimaginable to think that banks would collapse and entire industries would come grinding to a halt. The effect was that individuals who had been relying on income streams from those industries or cash tied up in the banks were left penniless and, in some cases, destitute. I love real estate (as you may have noticed), but it would be irresponsible and naïve of me to rely entirely on that as an income stream.

The great thing is that having numerous income streams in different sectors not only protects you against these changes and provides security for your family, but it will also grow your wealth exponentially.

These are the four different types of income:

Business
Business income is cash that comes to you as result of a business or asset that you own and a result of systems, assets, and people working for you.

Earned
Earned income relies on you being physically present to generate cash. This could be a job, being self-employed, speaking engagements, coaching, etc.

Leveraged
Leveraged income comes as a result of real estate investments and stock investments. These income streams, although still very leveraged, still require your presence and your time and input.

Hands-Free
Dividends, book royalties, royalties from patents and software, credit card cash back, interest earnings.

This isn't to say that you should start twenty things at once in some haphazard way and try to juggle them all. In fact, it's quite the opposite. It means making strategic, long-term decisions based on facts. It means following the 80:20 set and forget rule.

At first glance, the different types of income seem very separate and difficult to fit together, but quite the opposite is true. As you gain wealth, it is absolutely your priority and your responsibility to ensure you delve into, ideally, at least three of these income types.

Business Income

Business income is gained as a result of a company you own that has assets such as clients, tools, factories, facilities, staff, and intellectual property, and it generates revenue without you acting as a primary service provider. That's a long sentence, but its essence is this—if you lapsed into a coma, how long could your business run and generate revenue at its current level without you?

The reality, for most people, is not very long. Even if they don't have to be physically present on the factory line for the business to earn revenue, they haven't taken the time to develop real systems, train staff, or ensure that there are other leaders in place to continue the growth of the company and uninterrupted service to your clients. Serious business owners should also have adequate insurances in place—key man insurance, directors insurance—to ensure that every individual and the business as a whole is adequately protected.

While owning a massive multinational corporation might not appeal to you, the likely truth is that you have begun your quest to accrue wealth to gain more freedom, not less. Unless you wrap your head around the idea that you will need staff and you will need to become a leader, it will be a long, hard road. You may end up rich but you will not be wealthy. Wealth is about living, experiencing, having fun, and laughing. It's not about counting your gold bars and worrying about meeting KPIs.

If you are sitting there right now, reading this and realizing that you have a job and not a business, don't worry. You are not alone. Take heart—there are millions of people around the world that haven't even realized that yet and won't until they try to retire. Suddenly, this thing they have dedicated the best years of their life to, the thing they've loved and nurtured and looked after in hopes it would one day look after them, is worth a big fat *zero. Nada. Zilch.*

You see, the big value of a business is in its assets and systems. If *you* are those assets because you are the cleaner, the receptionist, the bookkeeper, and the cook, and the only systems you have are the ones that you know work best in your head, then the business has absolutely no value. There is nothing for anyone to buy. There is nothing anyone would *want* to buy. Although taking the time to train staff and produce training manuals and systems is hard work and time-consuming, a well-run business with those elements in place can be worth over ten times its annual revenue. Tasty, huh?

Even if your business isn't where you now know it needs to be, with some concerted effort in the right places, you can absolutely turn things around and extricate yourself from the business, thus giving yourself the luxury of selling it or enjoying its revenue.

Earned Income

Earned income requires your physical presence to generate money. This could be your day job or your self-employed business. It could even be public speaking, consulting, or mentoring. I'm going to assume for a moment that your main income stream is earned, and you work five to seven days a week. If you are self-employed or employed, chances are you work far too hard for way too little money. You're in a dangerous spiral that is detrimental to your health and your wealth, and it needs to change quickly.

Begin by writing down on a piece of paper everything you do during the day. Everything from switching the light on to mopping the bathroom to fulfilling orders for consumers. This simple act is the beginning of you creating assets which will turn your self-employed job into a business with value. With this list, you can begin to outsource all of the elements you either don't do well or don't enjoy doing. On first glance, this looks expensive. It looks like something you can't afford to do. But before you make assumptions, read step seven on leveraging and check out Chris Ducker's book, *Virtual Freedom*.

Whatever you have been doing up until now can be turned into an earned income stream. If you are employed as a web technician, you can begin freelancing. If you are a government employee, you will probably have fantastic skills managing people and working as part of a team, and that can be made into a training program or turned into a book and sold. These may not be your dream roles, but we are trying to help you create wealth in the shortest period of time. Finding creative ways to generate extra income, which can then be invested, really gets momentum on your side and can transform your life faster than you can imagine. Your earned income can and should still generate substantial cash. When I began public speaking, I initially gave talks to groups and organizations for free to hone my craft, gain exposure, and spread my message. Now, I charge thousands of dollars just for a few hours, and it's something I love doing!

The compound effect really starts to gain momentum when you can take the proceeds from one income stream and invest it into assets, which give you additional income. For example, one of my businesses is wholesale ecommerce, so we manufacture products for our health and lifestyle brand and sell them on ecommerce sites and to smaller retailers. This is a great business—it has massive cash flow with very few overheads and a forty percent profit margin. But markets and fashions change. History shows us that what people buy can change dramatically, even over only a few years. As a result, relying on that for income would be naïve. Instead, we take the profits and reinvest them—primarily into real estate. That way we are using profits from one business in a tax-efficient way to buy assets that will increase in value in the long term and generate cash flow. Pretty exciting.

On average, most millionaires have seven separate and unrelated streams of income. They build each of these one at a time using the set and forget strategy.

Leveraged Income

Leveraged income is sometimes called passive income, but this can be misleading. For an income stream to be truly passive, it should be hands-free and require no input from you at all. No one cares about you or your family like you do, right? The same applies to your assets. No one cares about your properties, businesses, or investments as much as you do, and that's not a bad thing or a reflection on you or them, it's just fact. As a result of this, you need to monitor your investments and your assets, carry out spot checks, and send in secret shoppers. It doesn't matter how you do it, but you need to make sure that the assets that nourish and look after you are also being nourished and looked after themselves. It can take as little as an hour per month, and there are some tips and tricks to help but that is the crucial difference that makes an income stream leveraged rather than passive.

Your real estate portfolio will become a leverage income stream. Once you have your team in place and the portfolio has been systemized using the 80:20 principle it will take very little of your time but still *some* input to monitor your manager.

Other leveraged income streams are business investments that you are either a shareholder in or maybe a non-executive director. You put in maybe a day a month to work with the team and oversee the strategy but your time is leveraged as you have people actually carrying out the day to day running of the business.

Once you have assets like real estate or a business investment, asking for copies of the last three months' inspections or reports will give you a great overview. It only takes an hour or so, but you can get an idea of where things are and which aspects might need support, and it will also allow you to provide some really great feedback and a pat on the back to the people who are doing a great job.

Other examples might be income from internet marketing/ banner advertising, dividends from business you are not involved in, potentially trading the markets if you are using software to automate it. All these business interests allow you to generate a great income with some input but no day to day hands on work.

Hands-Free Income

Hands-free income is everybody's favorite. This is income that is truly passive, it isn't earned. It doesn't depend on your actions, and it arrives in your bank account without you lifting a finger. This type of income stream includes dividends from bonds or interest from bank accounts, cash back on credit cards, pensions, and royalties.

While this kind of income stream is wonderful because it is hands-free, it is also unpredictable and should definitely not be relied upon. Many credit card companies and even bank accounts now provide cash back for money spent with them or money deposited. Bonds are often one of the long-term, low-risk investment strategies that you set and forget. Once a book is written, and you have completed the initial launch and moved on to creating other types of intellectual property, you rarely if ever have to promote it again, and thus it becomes hands-free. All of these strategies are great, but they are also out of your control. For example, at any time, your bank and credit card company may decide they no longer want to offer cash back—and your income is immediately reduced, perhaps significantly.

Network marketing is often coined as a hands-free set and forget business strategy, and it can be fantastic for generating income, but it should not be relied upon as a singular income stream for the same reasons as the credit card cash back—you are entirely at the mercy of other people to decide which commissions you get and whether they change their mind about it altogether.

These hands-free income strategies are all adjuncts to your other wealth-generating activities. The 80:20 set and forget enables you to continue growing income streams in a methodical manner that ensures you don't lose sight of the first business and don't get distracted by the shiny penny syndrome.

We aim to add one income stream per year to our businesses. As it stands, many are connected. For example, we have a rental/leasing business and a real estate maintenance company. These are great income generators. But because they are all interlinked, if there should be a big crash in the property market, there is a chance they will both suffer a drop in revenue at the same time. However, it is unlikely that the real estate companies and the wholesale business I own will suffer a dip. This is why having a variety of income streams is beneficial—it's an extra layer of security and protection for you and your family.

Sacrifice—Is It Worth It?

The common diatribe is that wealth is there for everyone, and anyone can achieve it. While that is technically true, it hides a really serious fact—not everyone who wants to achieve it will do so. Some just won't have the staying power or be prepared to pay the price for the wealth, and rest assured, there *is* a price.

"Entrepreneurship is living a few years of your life like most people won't, so that you can spend the rest of your life like most people can't." This anonymous quote speaks volumes about the price for wealth. As you begin to create wealth, you will probably find you are working harder than your peers—and probably with less disposable income because as they are giving in to instant gratification and consumerism and getting further into debt, you are saving and investing all of your funds. In the short term, you will be sacrificing shopping trips, holidays, new cars, and time. If your *why* isn't strong enough, and your will to leave a legacy isn't powerful enough, the sacrifice—for you—will not be worth it.

Action Steps

Remember the wealthy get rich because of the things they say no to, not the things they say yes to. Choose a strategy, put everything into it. Front load your mistakes and fail your way to success. Use the 80:20 principle. Build a team, create systems and strategies. Set the first strategy and then move on to creating your next income stream.

Share ideas for creating systems and building teams in the Freedom Property Academy

www.freedompropertyacademy.com/membership-home-page/community/

Chapter Six

Step 6 Partnerships

Partnerships are the most underutilized but most powerful tool there is available. If you want to take your wealth and/or your business to the next level, the quickest way to do that is to partner with other people and businesses.

Partnerships abound, and you probably haven't even noticed them yet. You see companies everywhere paying millions of dollars to advertise at sporting events and on reality TV shows. Farmers partner with stores to sell their milk and meat, and they share in the profit. Partnerships were around long before we invented fancy terms like joint ventures, and yet the majority of the world still isn't using them. There is the idea floating around that everybody out there is in competition. That everybody wants to steal your thoughts and your clients. It's a ridiculous notion, and it comes from a place of scarcity and fear, not wealth and abundance. There are literally billions of people in the world, and each one has different needs and attractions. Rather than compete with all of these other people, why not partner with them and let the clients decide who best serves their needs.

The easiest way to think about partnerships is by imagining two people with contrasting skills sharing resources. This might include a partnership between a great copywriter and a website designer—the web guy can do his thing, creating amazing pieces of artwork for the computer, and the copy guy can write words that drip like melted chocolate and draw people in. Each person can advertise the services of the other to their audience and agree on a win-win profit share. By using this method, they have both reached an audience for FREE that they wouldn't have had otherwise, and they have increased both their mailing lists and their revenues. Pretty cool concept!

So how does this apply to you? As you begin your journey to wealth, most of your challenges will likely come under a couple of banners. Whether you overcome these challenges will depend on one thing, and one thing only. What or whom do you bring to the table?

All partnerships must be a triple win by nature—a win for you, a win for your partner, and a win for the people you serve. Looking at it another way, consider this book as an example. You may have bought it on Amazon Kindle. How exactly did that happen? Amazon invested billions in creating a fantastic bit of technology that lets you read books anywhere without having to lug a cumbersome tome around. They figured out a way to make their product light up but not reflect the sun into your face. They then integrated this with an already awesome ecommerce site with a great search engine which enabled you to find this book. And Kindle is integrated with the checkout and payment gateway so the book can be delivered in one click straight to your Kindle device. Awesome.

Now, I had two options. I could try to invent something that does the same thing as Kindle, competing with Amazon for sales to make it profitable for me, and then trying to persuade other publishers to use my technology—which, frankly, would probably be inferior and much higher-priced because I don't have economies of scale. Or I could choose to partner with Amazon and other e-publishers. And that's what I did. I stuck to what I do best—which is sharing my experiences and training people in how to create wealth—and wrote this guide to success. I then sent it to Amazon, at which point I let them do what they do best—get it to you!

When you start looking for partnerships, consider what assets you already have, both tangible and intangible. An example of a tangible asset might be a mailing list or money, and an intangible asset could include a great track record of successful JVs or your education after becoming a trained investor.

To get you started, here is a list of tangible and intangible assets.

Which of these do you have? What other assets do you have? Start creating your list of assets that you can use to approach and attract JV partners.

- Honest
- Difference market
- Good Credit Score
- Ethical Marketing
- Knowledge
- Specific skills e.g.
- Trustworthy Audience
- Experience
- Mailing List
- Reliable
- Training
- Opposing skills
- Hard Working
- Time rich
- Vitality / Energy
- Cash available
- Connections
- Track Record

Remember, you need to know what you bring to the table to be an attractive JV partner and create a win-win partnership. On your journey to true wealth, your challenges will likely come under one of two banners: 1) Not enough money or 2) Not enough knowledge or experience. At the moment, these might seem insurmountable, but I assure you, they are not!

Cash Joint Venture

Let's start with money first. Why would cash-rich people want to partner with you? The answer? Because they absolutely need to. Anyone with a pot of money must do a couple of things. Initially, they need to diversify to spread their risk. Then they need to be getting a return. As long as their money just sits in the bank—especially at a time of such low interest rates—they are literally losing money.

For example, if an investor has $100K in the bank, earning him 1% per year, at the end of year one, he will, in theory, have $101K. However, if during that same time, inflation was at five percent, his money would be eroded by $5K. So at the end of the first year, his initial $100K is now only worth $96K ($100,000 + $1,000 = $101,000 - $5,000 = $96k). Imagine if those figures were larger. Suddenly, vast proportions of his wealth are being lost or not realized, year after year.

Now in that same example, what if you took his $100K and invested it in real estate that earned him 10% per year. What would the figures look like then? At the end of year one, his $100K would be $110k. His net worth has increased.

At the time I began investing, I didn't even know there were people who had $100K just sitting around. It was completely out of my realm of understanding, and even when mentors (and it took a few!) tried to convince me otherwise, I really didn't believe a thing they said. Here's the truth: There is an estimated $70 trillion currently in the world, and there are seven billion people. There is more than enough money. Imagine money as a fluid substance that travels to where activity and value is greatest. You just don't have your share yet. When you add some value to the world, you are financially rewarded in proportion. Mark Zuckerburg and Facebook, for example, serve and add value to one billion people daily and are so compensated. If you start to consider money as nothing more than a measure of value that you put out into the world, it becomes a much less daunting prospect.

Most of my initial wealth came through real estate, and although I was earning well, it wasn't until I really starting adding value to the world that my net worth increased exponentially. For me, adding value took the shape of employing my tenants who were previously on welfare and of having a fantastic standard of shared housing at a time when local standards were appalling. We had a list of tenants waiting, we had councils and charities desperate to work with us, and we had an incredibly profitable but beneficial enterprise. This isn't an anomaly. Look at all the wealthy people you see in the papers—all the business leaders and the personal development leaders are producers. They have books and programs and businesses. Money follows the industrious. It likes activity.

Realizing now that money flows to industry and activity, you have to be brutally honest with yourself. What are you doing to earn and attract money?

Answer the following questions:

- Have you been networking?
- Have you found some deals/investments that need cash?
- Have you been telling other professionals what you do?
- Have you been to a seminar?
- Have you read a book or listened to an audio book?

If you answered *no* to these, the really important question I need to ask you is *Why not?* What is stopping you from taking action?

Confidence Versus Competence

Most often, the answer is confidence. At least 99% of my clients will say to me that they haven't been to a conference, been networking, or conducted a viewing with a realtor because they don't know anything, and they don't want to look stupid or silly.

This is an interesting statement because in the early stages of learning any skill, confidence comes from competence. If you don't feel like you are good at something, you won't feel confident. Fair enough. However, if you then don't take action educate yourself and learn the skills, how are you ever going to feel confident enough to get out there and make it happen? You won't. And now we have come full circle.

You want more money, and you want to live wealthy, yet you don't have the competence to do something about it and don't have the confidence to attend a seminar and change that. Scarier than looking a bit silly once should be the idea of never living the life of your dreams because of your fears. Personally, I can live with looking like an idiot. I can live with failing. But I can't live with not trying. My life force, the reason I get out of bed every day, is to try to be better so that I can serve more people. If I take that away, I can't breathe. I'm suffocating.

So how do you break that cycle? Start small. There are so many fantastic books available now on creating wealth, investing ethically, and real estate investing. So buy just one book—and read it. You are now ahead of at least fifty percent of the population. Research shows that, on average, forty-two percent of people did not read a nonfiction book in the last year. Of those who did, at least fifty percent of them did not finish the book. Just the act of reading and finishing that one book gives you more knowledge that 99% of your circle. And here's the really exciting thing. Remember when we were goal setting, I told you that how you got there didn't matter? This is when that kicks in. You don't need to know how you're going to get all the knowledge you need, you just need take a step in the right direction.

Imagine you continue on that path for six months, reading a couple of books a month. Maybe you listen to a podcast and buy an online training program or attend a seminar as well. Will that make you an educated investor? Absolutely! Do you then have something to offer a JV partner? For sure.

You see, the funny thing about the normal working guy with a high-paying job who has money to invest is that he is usually working so hard earning his money that he doesn't have the time, energy, or brain capacity to find ways to invest it sensibly. Therefore, they need ethical and educated investors to partner with.

There is a common question that I usually hear next. Why would they want to invest with *me* when they can choose from anyone?

Was I right? Is that what you're thinking?

People Buy from People

I'll let you in on another secret it took me years to figure out. *People buy from people.* You're absolutely right. There are a million places people can put their cash, but in how many of those places can they sit down, look someone in the eyes, and decide if they're a good person? How often do they meet a person who has done the work, taken the time to get educated, and is now offering attractive, strategic, and specific investment opportunities?

Have you ever bought something from a salesman that you had absolutely no intention of buying before? A few years ago, I popped into a well-known electrical retail store to look at something (I can't even remember what it was now), and I walked out of that store with a laptop, a printer, a laptop bag, and a whole bunch of other stuff I didn't even need! Why? Because I trusted the salesman. He knew his products, he was able to match me to something I liked, and eventually, I wanted it. Ultimately, I bought into *him.*

It's no different for you. If you're likeable and know what you're talking about, you are educated and have done the research, and you can make an appropriate, ethical, and profitable investment offering, people will have no reason to go anywhere else.

I can't emphasize this point enough. When I began investing, I was homeless. I didn't even have a house, and yet I was expecting other people to invest with me to buy other people's homes. I had no confidence, no experience, and no money to bring to the table. Wherever you are right now, you are likely in a better position than I was. I couldn't get my head around it at the time, but I had completely misjudged the value I brought, and this is exactly what I share with people I train now. *You* are the value. You are the asset. The fact that you are even bothering to read this book and start to learn the possibilities that are out there for you tells me you are a person of value. There are enough books and people promising that you can get rich quick through scams and by ripping people off. You wouldn't need to read this if that is what you want, but it's not. You're attracted to this book because, like me, you want to do things the right way and be the best you possibly can, and that, my friend, is priceless.

The magic to all of this is that you get to be *YOU!* You don't need to pretend to have loads of experience or millions of dollars. You can act with honesty, decency, and congruency to your values and beliefs. All you need is to learn is to value yourself and your knowledge properly and then position it in a way that gets above the noise, and investors will buy into you.

In case you're wondering, I owned eight houses before I moved out the physical therapy office—I was possibly the wealthiest homeless person ever!

You have to remember that this is a win-win, long-term relationship—and not just in talk. Talk, as they say, is cheap. Approach everything you do with a view to creating results that are a win for everyone. Warren Buffet said, "It takes twenty years to build a reputation and five minutes to ruin it. If you think about that, you'll do things differently." And boy, was he right! No amount of short-term profit is worth the risk of ruining the one thing on which you build your entire career. People forgive and forget mistakes, but they don't forgive or forget deception easily.

You are offering a great investment opportunity with—if you are doing it the right way—a great profit return potential. You are offering your time, knowledge, and education. All of this is valuable and should be factored in when figuring out what you bring to the table. Desperation doesn't win trust. Recognize your value and never lower your standards. After I had been investing for a year, I was offered a $2.5m investment from a very wealthy investor, but he wasn't prepared to acknowledge the work I had done by building a team in my chosen investment area, researching the area, building a local presence, and gaining education and experience. Ultimately, it would not have been win-win for me. Turning that cash down was the hardest thing I had ever had to do in my professional life, but I was not prepared to lower my standards, and neither should you.

Now let's look at partnering with someone with more experience.

Experience/Skills Joint Venture

Let's flip the situation a little bit and check out the landscape if you happen to be the one with the cash—or at least some of the cash—and you would like to partner with someone who brings knowledge and experience to the table. Maybe you are ready to invest in real estate but, rather than taking it all on yourself, the first thing you would like to do is bring a trusted partner on board.

This is a really great strategy, and something I still use and recommend. The real value in this is created when you choose the partner. Before you even begin looking, you need to be really clear on what you want from the partnership. For example, do you want just a financial return and emailed updates, or do you want to be knee-deep in the strategic planning and meetings?

There isn't a right or a wrong way, but it must meet your needs and those of the right partner. Let's look at this practically:

Example One

Jenni owns a florist shop. She's forty-four and has two teenage children. She would like to invest in real estate to build a portfolio for her pension, but she's too busy to learn how to do it strategically and isn't really interested in how it all works. She just wants to diversify her income and get a better return on her money.

Jenni meets Neil at a local networking meeting for business owners. Neil has been investing for around ten years with a lot of success. He can prove all of his results and passes all the due diligence tests with flying colors. He's a great guy, and they hit it off right away. Neil attends the meetings because working from home gets lonely, and he really wants people to share the journey with and bounce ideas off of. Although most people in that area could offer a ten percent annual return, Neil will return 7.5% because he's willing to share his secrets to success and show people how to do it.

Do they seem a good fit? On the face of it, yes. They are two great people doing their thing. They meet and complete all the due diligence and have great fun doing it, so they know working together wouldn't be a problem. So what *is* the problem? Go back and recall that Jenni doesn't want to get involved—she just wants a great hands-free return. It might work well in the beginning, but as soon as the novelty wears off, she'll remember why she didn't have time in the first place and will start to retreat. This will probably be compounded by her not achieving the returns she could have if she'd worked with someone else. Neil, in turn, will be frustrated because he isn't getting the interaction and support he was after. If they aren't careful, the situation could become really unpleasant just because two great people feel a bit let down in their expectations.

Example Two

Sam has $150,000 available to invest in real estate. He is fairly flexible about the terms of the investment and return, but he really wants to do more real estate, so learning on the job is important to him. He reaches out to his network to ask if anyone is looking for financial investment or knows someone who is. He receives two credible proposals back.

Proposal A: Mr. Wilson is a multimillionaire. He has a number of businesses, including a large-scale development business converting casinos, leisure centers, and so on. As the leader of the organizations, he makes strategic decisions but stays out of the everyday operations. He has a great development that could use the funding. He can provide one percent per month for eight months and a personal guarantee.

Proposal B: Miss Parker has just completed her third refurbishment. Each time, the scale of the project has increased, and she is now renovating a large house. She is a full-time investor and manages the refurbishments herself. Although she has some cash reserves, a personal guarantee would be useless in real terms. The deal can pay 0.75% per month and will last twelve to fifteen months.

Which would you advise Sam to go with? Hopefully, Miss Parker. Sam was clear that his primary goal was to learn, and he is prepared to invest time and accept a lower return to do that. Although the deal offered by Mr. Wilson is pretty good, he will be far too busy to invest any time with Sam and, in reality, will have a team of architects, lawyers, accountants, quantity surveyors, and the like working for him. In contrast, Miss Parker is completely invested in making her one project a success. She will oversee each and every aspect and attend all meetings with planners and other members of the team. She will be on site as much as possible. She will also likely enjoy the company and shared experience, so it will truly be a win-win. From a purely financial standpoint, if Sam invested with Mr. Wilson, he would receive an eight percent return and would then need to get his money working for him again. Investing with Miss Parker will take longer, but he will end up with an 11.25% return, lots of knowledge, and more time to find his next project.

In both examples, clarity in what they were looking for from a partnership would avoid some uncomfortable conversations. Let's not forget, just because someone isn't the right partner for you doesn't mean you can't be friends and take the relationship further on a footing that works for everyone. But here's the thing…creating wealth and financial freedom can either be a really profitable business or a really expensive hobby. You want to create business relationships and become a leader. Turning partnerships down may not be comfortable, but your wealth and your future will likely be determined by the things you say *no* to, not the things you say *yes* to.

When you are considering your value in a partnership, remember this.

Have you ever had a single friend who was down in the dumps because they didn't know why anyone wouldn't like them? Within ten seconds, you could reel off twenty reasons why that friend is amazing and why someone would be lucky to have them. Well, this is you. You are sitting on a mountain of value that manifests in many different ways, but until you recognize that, you can't expect anyone else to.

So you've found someone you think is a good fit for a partnership. Now what?

First of all, breathe! If you've ever been to a conference, networking meeting, or seminar before, you will undoubtedly have seen the people running around with brochures, trying to collect as many business cards as possible and sell to everyone unfortunate enough to be caught next to them. This rarely, if ever, works. We've just explored that people do business with people they like. We as humans buy into people, not products. Bearing that in mind takes massive pressure off meetings and events. Your only goal is to create relationships that you can subsequently follow up on.

Get a Partnership 'Through not To'

The most effective way to get an 'in' and arrange a first meeting is to use a tool called TNT—Through not To. Imagine you're looking for finance. You have an investment strategy or a business, and you need the cash to get going. Asking up front is awkward and uncomfortable for everyone. If you ask outright and get turned down, it can knock your confidence (which should be treated like gold dust until you find your feet). Equally, you put the other person in an uncomfortable position, and they will usually say no right away because no one really likes being put on the spot.

So to get around it, you sell *through* them. A few minutes into your conversation, you will ask them what brought them to the event and what they're hoping to gain from it, to which they will probably tell you whatever comes to mind because, unlike you, they won't have a great pitch ready. They will most likely reciprocate with, "What are you looking for?" And this is when you reply, "I have a fantastic business proposal that I've worked really hard on, I have a mentor and the experience and drive to succeed, and I'm looking for a great joint venture partner who might want to invest. So if you know anyone who would like a twenty percent return on their money over a year with ten percent equity, please feel free to connect us."

How awesome is that? You have completely taken the heat out of the situation while still fully explaining what you have to offer. If they are interested themselves, you will see it. They may even express some interest in having you mail them some information. If not, they'll say something like, "I don't know anyone right now, but I'll definitely keep that in mind." Without selling yourself out and feeling exposed or pouncing on the first person who stops by, you have pitched to them (and whoever else was within earshot). It's such a powerful tool, and it has raised me hundreds and hundreds of thousands of dollars in partnership finance. You would be surprised how many people will tell you that they're not interested, but their mom, sister, or friend might be!

Even the biggest introvert can use this because you aren't asking for anything and you aren't making yourself vulnerable. It's relaxed but structured. You can and should practice it so it just rolls off your tongue each and every time you use it.

Pitching for Partners

The most powerful tool you have in your arsenal is a show-stopping pitch. This isn't a pitch that you want to end in a sale, but rather a relationship pitch. Essentially, it's a powerful tool that puts your best foot forward and lets the other person understand very quickly who you are and what you can offer.

I was at a meeting a few days ago and a guy I'd spotted an hour or so earlier came shuffling up and hovered uncomfortably behind me. At the time I was in a circle having a group chat, so joining in wouldn't have been difficult. After a moment, I introduced myself and asked him what he did. His reply was something along the lines of "Umm, I uhhh, my name's David, and I, umm, am hopefully going to probably, umm, buy a house to sort of, um, rent out, I guess." Okay, that might be a slight exaggeration, but you get my point. After some digging, I found that he had actually completed one of my trainings, had raised some joint venture finance, and was now looking for his first real estate investment. I was very impressed with his accomplishment in such a short time and was able to connect him with some people in his area, and they are now looking at working together.

So he impressed me, but I had to work hard for it. How much more powerful would it have been if he had walked up to the group, stood next to me and smiled, and then said, "Hi Kemi, we haven't met yet, but I'm Dave. I've completed your program and put it into action. I know you have a big network, so if you do know anyone in X area that is looking for a friend in business, would you mind connecting us?"

Where Do You Meet Joint Venture Partners?

Chances are, if you are interested in something—be it real estate, forex, stocks, or entrepreneurship—there are other people in your network who are also interested, so reach out to them and arrange to have coffee and chat about your plans. You may find there is some synergy there, and you can explore that further. Or they might connect you with someone else who is interested.

Moth or The Flame

Robert Kiyosaki said, "Your network is equal to your net worth." This is so true. The truly wealthy have friends who are also their peers. The wealthy know how to create relationships with influencers and leaders.

We need to surround ourselves with like-minded people who are striving, aiming to achieve more, and living their lives to the fullest. Having this kind of powerful network will not only make networking and finding suitable partnerships a lot easier, but it will also lift the level at which you're playing. Many of the great self-development experts say that you are the average of the five people you spend the most time with. Does that thought scare you or excite you?

There are two ways of creating a network. You can be the moth, or you can be the flame.

The Moth.

Moths flutter around in a seemingly haphazard way, bumping into things. Some of the things they bump into are great, some not so great, but they float around from room to room, just seeing what happens.

In networking terms, moths are people who attend groups at random. They don't have a real strategy and just see what comes along. They definitely have some success and will almost always be great with people, easily working a room and networking confidently.

The Flame.

The flame of a candle is strong and alluring. Humans can be like candles. People are attracted to them, and they are the center of most social events. People are talking about them and trying to be near them. They are influencers.

Influencers don't just attend networking events and meet-ups, they *create* them. A great tip if you want to be the flame is to tell everyone you know that you are arranging a meet in a local bar—or wherever—for everyone interested in real estate, and they should come along and bring anyone they know who is also interested. The first time, it may just be two or three of you, but the next month, that'll grow to seven or eight and so on. The best part of this strategy is that you are the center of it all. The question everyone is asking is "How do you know so-and-so?" As a result, you very quickly form your own circle of influence, and anytime someone mentions real estate, who do you think will come to mind and be recommended to them? Yep. You.

There is nothing wrong with being either the moth or the flame. It may depend on your personality type and also time availability. If you are very busy and time is limited, becoming the flame and organizing meetings close to your home may be the way to move forward. You will often find you develop closer relationships faster than when you are the moth. On the flip side, the moth will know lots of people everywhere and will pop up in conversations all around your town.

So which are you going to be, the Moth or the Flame?

Where else can you meet joint venture partners?

Networking Meetings

Networking meetings are increasingly common, as are business support networks. Attending these is a great first step in building a peer group of like-minded people to help you on your quest to create wealth and make a difference. MeetUp.Com is a great site for common interest meetings and finding other people who are also interested in entrepreneurship and business.

Another easy way to find meetings is simply to Google your keyword (i.e. Real Estate) + networking + your town

Seminars

I personally have met a lot of joint venture partners at seminars. In that environment, you are guaranteed to meet people who have invested time and money into their future. If your circumstances allow, try to attend higher-priced seminars and conferences—people who have invested a substantial amount aren't messing around! Remember not to spend the whole time talking to the people you arrived with, and memorize your introduction pitch beforehand and use the 'Through Not To' tool to spread the word about the great work you are doing.

LinkedIn

What an incredible tool, and it's free! I don't know of any other tool that is as cost and time efficient and allows you to connect directly with the movers and shakers of any industry. There is even a bio and a list of interests to make breaking the ice and finding common ground to connect with someone so easy.

Top Tip: When you send an invitation to connect, customize it. Make sure you thank the person for their time, compliment them on something you admire, and don't offer or sell anything. Though leaders and experienced people get hundreds of LinkedIn invites, most people don't bother to customize, and even if they do, it will only be to ask for something. Remember that we're going for relationships not sales. Imagine how much difference it would make if someone connected with you by sending a message that said something like:

"Hey ——,

I just wanted to connect after reading your latest article on Leadership. As with all your work, it had some great points that I've been able to take action on already. If I can do anything to help just give me a shout."

Wouldn't that get your attention over this:

"I would like to invite you to connect."

Or worse, this:

"Hi Dave,

I see that you're interested in real estate. I have some investments that need funding. Are you interested? Call me on........."

They're worlds apart, aren't they? The first guy already has your attention and respect. He has flattered your ego a little bit, made you feel appreciated, and then offered to help. That's a pretty great footing to start off any relationship, and if you look at it, isn't subservient. There's no ass kissing or sucking up. Just an appreciation of work and mutual respect.

Remember: LinkedIn is not Facebook. No one cares what you had for dinner or whether your dog barks along to songs on the radio. This is a professional engagement platform designed for you to display your knowledge and skills, not share the bits of you that only your best friends should know about!

Social Media

Social media like Facebook and Twitter are great tools for sharing what you are achieving to a wide audience and connecting with people that you previously wouldn't have gotten near.

Facebook

As you probably know, Facebook lets you update your status and post videos and pictures of what you are up to. Most people use it to let the world know what kind of pasta they had for dinner or how much they hate parking attendants. When the world goes one way, you should go the other. While everybody else is mindlessly rambling, you can share what book you are reading (feel free to give this one a shout out!), which conferences you have been attending, and any learnings you have acquired.

After a few months of really honing your skills and learning your trade, you should have a great investment strategy and a potential opportunity. You can then update your status with a brief introduction to the opportunity and the profit you expect to achieve—again selling *through not to.* Your status might say something like "Really excited to find this off-market real estate opportunity. Comparable sales in the area show we're going to be buying it for 15% below market value, and we can add an extra 20% to that, so there's around $70k profit to be made. Next step is narrowing down which joint venture partner to do this with." There's every chance no one will raise their hand at this point, but as you carry on your project with other investment partners, keep updating your status, and when the next opportunity is posted, watch your inbox fill up.

In essence, you want to be using Facebook to show your skills and knowledge in an approachable and exciting way.

Twitter

Twitter has limited the number of characters you have available to 140. Rather than a negative, this gives you the opportunity to really stand out above the crowd. Use your bio to demonstrate your authority, and use your updates to again show what you are up to. Hash tags are fantastic as well for finding people who are talking about your interest. Use the search bar at the top to enter #keyword and then join in the conversation. Again, engage with thoughtful leaders. Compliment them on their work and retweet anything that you relate to or you think your followers might appreciate. Gradually build up relationships.

If you build a relationship and then see they are coming to a town near you, you could offer to recommend a hotel or restaurant and then mention that a coffee would be great. Just keep giving value before you ask for anything.

How to Avoid Bad Joint Venture Partners

Only Partner with People You Like

I'd love to tell you that all joint venture partnerships—or for that matter, all businesses—always go smoothly and nothing ever goes wrong, but that would be disingenuous of me. Sometimes things don't go according to plan. Unexpected challenges arise, or maybe someone just messes up. The most important thing is to get used to it because it will happen. I'm glad because I learn far more from the things that go wrong than from the things that go right. With that in mind, however, if things do go wrong, you need to be able to have a conversation with your joint venture partner over a drink and be honest. "Look, X has happened and, because of that, it's going to take an extra week, or the returns will be 9.5% and not 10.5% as predicted. I have come up with these three possible solutions. I recommend solution B. How do you feel? Are you happy with that?"

If your joint venture partner is someone you don't feel you could have an honest chat with, then absolutely do not do business with them. I promise you will regret it and, honestly, so will they.

Put Everything in Writing

This is a common oversight when you get going, especially if you're working with friends or family members. In that instance, it's often assumed that each person will do as agreed, and it will all just happen. It isn't the case very often that people intend to mislead. But we all live busy lives, your JV partners are busy as well, and there is every chance that there were assumptions made or things misunderstood. If everything is in writing, all vagueness is removed from the equation.

Communication is a skill, and it takes time and training to learn to listen. Often when people are quiet, they are just waiting for an opportunity to speak again rather than actually listening to the message behind your words. You can be sure that what you said and what the other person heard are not the same thing. Having an agreement in writing avoids any later confusion or possibility for disagreements. It doesn't need to be a $10,000 legal agreement, just a simple agreement with the terms, what is expected from each person, and brief timelines.

Under-Promise and Over-Deliver

You know how good you are and what you can potentially deliver, but nothing ruins credibility like failing to deliver. There is no need to put yourself at risk of losing credibility—especially after all your hard work to earn it—and no need to put yourself under even greater pressure by promising the world. If your opportunity is decent, then most serious joint venture partners will be interested. If you can hit all your targets and deliver more than they expected, you will come out of it looking superhuman, and they'll respect you even more. It's often forgotten that when you form a partnership, you are utilizing an underused resource that the partner already has. If that resource is money, they may be getting only one percent per year in the bank, so a six percent investment is a 600% increase. Do you think they'll be delighted if you can offer that? Oh yes!

But if you offer them fourteen percent, you run the risk of it looking too good to be true, possibly losing credibility even if the investment can carry that kind of return. And if you promise fourteen percent but deliver only eight percent—even if it's 800% more than they were getting—are they going to be pleased? Possibly. More than likely, any feelings of pleasure will be tinged with disappointment and a feeling of being let down. On the flip side, if you offer six percent and deliver eight percent, they will be your best friend for life! Okay, maybe not your best friend, but do you think they'll have any problems investing with you again? Absolutely not. Better than that, they'll run around telling everyone that this person they know promised six percent but then delivered eight—and you'll have a line out the door of people wanting to work with you.

Alignment of Values

This is perhaps the single, most important factor in deciding who to joint venture with. Does the person value the same things as you? Will they put doing the right thing over an extra bit of profit? Are you both engaged with wanting to make a difference *and* a profit? Do they act with genuine, authentic congruency? Are they just 'good people'? You're not looking for the next Mother Theresa, although that would be nice, but you are looking for a decent, honest person you can work with to grow both your businesses and your wealth.

P.O.W.E.R Joint Venture Model

Use the Freedom Academy's P.O.W.E.R Joint Venture Model before going into any partnership.

P—Plan.

Do you have a strategic plan to appeal to potential joint venture partners? Once you have their interest, do you then have a professional, appropriate, profitable, and ethical business offering?

O—Opposing Skills/Resources.

Have you approached joint venture partners with the potential to add some value that you don't already have? Have you identified and demonstrated the value that you are bringing to the partnership? If you are looking for experience and mentoring during a project, approaching other inexperienced partners is unlikely to create a successful partnership.

W - Wants/Wins.

When we start any project, there is always something we want from it. Maybe we want to earn more money, raise our profile, learn new skills, increase our network, or raise money for charity. Let's say you want to joint venture with some speakers to increase your network and raise money for charity. When you are planning the project, you might say that by the end of the seminar you want to have an extra five experts in your network as you will invite them to speak and you will have raised $10,000 for charity from the proceeds of ticket sales. Achieving those things will be a win for you. Now let's imagine a win for your joint venture partner is earning $10,000 personally from ticket sales and raising his profile by being the main speaker throughout the seminar. You can already see that the two 'wins' don't align. Ensuring that your wants and wins are compatible is essential for a successful partnership.

E—Exits.

Particularly important in financial partnerships are the proposed exit(s) for either party. If you are arranging a short-term financial partnership, you need to have a minimum of two but ideally three exit plans. In real estate, you often buy houses to refurbish and then resell for a profit. That is one exit strategy. A second exit strategy would be ensuring that if the house doesn't sell, the amount the house would rent for is more than the mortgage and maintenance costs—a process called making sure it washes its face. This aligns closely with Wants/Wins if your partner is looking for a short-term profit and not a long-term business venture that might not bring any profits for three to six months and there is no exit prior to being in profit is not a good partnership.

R—Relationship

If you're an entrepreneur, and you're driven to changing your life and making a difference in the world like me (if you're reading this you probably are), you will enjoy talking about business, strategies, and plans. I'm fortunate enough to spend time with millionaires and hugely successful business owners, and we are constantly throwing ideas around, mulling thoughts over, and having impromptu mastermind sessions. When I ask what is the single most important factor in their success, every single one of those wealthy entrepreneurs, business owners, and investors has listed this next point as one of their top three:

ONLY DO BUSINESS WITH PEOPLE YOU LIKE.

The truth is that if you like a person, he or she is more than likely a good person with great ethics trying to do good business. Never underestimate your gut feeling. If your gut, the deepest part of your intuition, is telling you not to like someone or something, there's more than good reason for that. Remember that over thousands of years, all we've had to rely on is our gut to keep us safe from harm or threat. It is a developed and honed feeling about what we should or should not be doing. Guilt works in the same way. If you're feeling guilty about something on your moral compass, it's your gut telling you it's not the right thing to do.

As much as I'd love to tell you that everything in every partnership goes brilliantly and nothing ever goes wrong, it would be wrong of me to not prepare you and be honest about the fact that things *do* happen. If you've followed the P.O.W.E.R model, it doesn't need to be a catastrophe. Because you and your partner are coming at things from the same place and with the same goals, you can work together to find a solution. Relationship is crucial to that. You need to have an open, honest relationship based on mutual respect which allows you to enjoy your successes and work through challenges together.

Habits of the Wealthy

Who do you show up as?

"Dress and conduct yourself for the position you want, not the one you have."

It may be judgmental, and it may not be very nice, but the fact is humans are visual creatures. We judge things based on what we can see. We decide whether a meal will be good before we've even tasted it. We decide if we like a car based on its color rather than its function. And most of all, we judge other people based on looks and what our belief system says about their appearance. For example, if someone has a young appearance, and they tell you they are CEO of a big company, our internal voice kicks in and questions these statements because what we know of the world doesn't support the fact that this young person can be a CEO. In the same vein, if someone is dressed scruffily and looks a little disheveled but starts talking about their wealth, you are unlikely to believe or trust them because their appearance doesn't match your idea of what success should look like.

In the early days of creating wealth, your biggest challenge will be your mind. Everything you know about yourself and your life will be telling you that you're not going to create massive wealth. While you are pushing yourself to overcome hurdles and challenges, you will have that little voice in the back of your mind saying, "An investor? You're broke! What are you talking about?" or "Who's going to believe in you and give you a chance? You haven't achieved anything." Whatever your personal demons are, you are not alone. Each person, no matter how successful, will still be coping with their own baggage. The real test is not whether or not you have demons, but what you do about them.

An easy win for peace of mind is to dress for the job you want, and not for the job you have. By dressing smartly, you will instantly feel better about yourself, and the image you will project onto others is one of success. Each time those doubts come creeping in, go and look in the mirror. See how fine you look, and then ask yourself if someone unsuccessful would dress like that. It's a powerful way to override your mind.

So what message are your clothes giving out?

In most cases, it doesn't take money to make a big transformation—just a little bit of presentation. Make sure your clothes are clean and ironed, your shoes are polished, and your hair is cut and combed. You only get one chance to make a first impression. Imagine if you had the opportunity to pitch an idea to Richard Branson or Bill Gates. How would you dress?

Unless you have a manual day job that doesn't allow you to dress professionally, the quickest way to increase your wealth is to get a raise in your current position. Showing your employer you take your role seriously and add a lot of value to add to the organization is a fantastic way to get a raise.

Perception really is reality. As they say, if it looks like a duck and walks like a duck… If you do not have the appearance of someone who can be a leader or a manager, there is no chance your employer—or anyone else, for that matter—is ever going to recognize you as one.

FEAR

As you go through the journey of wealth creation and real estate, you will move onto bigger, more exciting, and more challenging projects. And each time, those voices will appear from nowhere and start telling you, "I know you pulled off the last one, but there's no way you can do this." Knowing that you have and will likely always have those voices is vital. More important is knowing what those voices are. They are *FEAR*. Those nagging doubts, questions, and ridicule that you hear are your deepest fears coming out and to say hello. So let's deal with those fears now.

Fear, although frustrating, isn't always a bad thing. Throughout time, there have been various threats to humans—heat, cold, bigger animals, lack of food, violence, lack of water, lack of shelter. We acquire fears based on what we know to be true, and despite the aforementioned fears not being legitimate or current fears for most of us lucky enough to live in the developed world, we still have those genetic fears engrained in our DNA. Given the right circumstances, they rear their ugly heads. Fortunately for us, for the most part, our fears lie dormant.

But in recent years, we have learned to fear disappointment, ridicule, and being told no. While none of these feelings are pleasant, they do not threaten harm to our lives. But in addition to these, what are the common fears people share with me where their pursuit of wealth is concerned?

Common Fear: What If I try for wealth and my dream life, and I fail?

You have only failed once you quit. At sixty-five, a man was living in his car, flat broke, and surviving on welfare checks of $99. Do you consider him a failure? He made a decision that he had to change. He pitched an idea 1,008 times, and each time it was rejected. Is he still a failure? On his 1,009th pitch, he got a yes. Ten years later, he sold his interest in his company for $2m ($15m in today's value). His name? Colonel Sanders, the founder of KFC. Is he still a failure?

The risk of failure is not only very real and very scary, it's very exciting. Yes, of course some people become billionaires at age twenty-one because of some tech startup, but the rest of us must fail our way to success. Each time you feel like you have failed, make a note to yourself that it's one failure closer to success. If I told you that you had to fail 100 times before you became a millionaire, how quickly would you start failing? Pretty quickly, I'd bet! Failure doesn't need to be catastrophic. It's part of the journey, and when you appreciate that, the failures are much easier to accept.

Most people with this fear are actually wondering…

Common Fear: What will my friends/family/significant other think of me if I fail?

Honestly, not a lot! Humans are far too selfish and self-involved, especially those that are working nine-to-five trying to survive and make ends meet, to think about you very much at all. Even if they do, what other people think about you is none of your business! Be always more concerned with how you feel about yourself. If you have conducted yourself well, been ethical, carried out due diligence, and worked hard, and something hasn't worked, then there's not a lot you can do about that. Interestingly, if you listen to most successful people talk, they will tell you that each time something hasn't worked out, they have learned something valuable that has created wealth for them in the future.

In the early days of your wealth building, I advise you to limit those in your inner circle with whom you share your plans. I know this goes against the grain with most 'experts', but I'll explain why I say this. It isn't because you are doing anything that you should be ashamed of. Quite the opposite. But the natural instinct of those who love you is to be scared for you. What you are doing is amazing and extraordinary, but for those without the same mindset and determination, it's scary as hell. When you are putting everything you have into creating a new life for yourself and your family, it doesn't help to have too many people sharing their fears with you. What you need is to create a group of peers. Some friends, acquaintances, and people in your new circle of influence—people who are all trying to do the same thing. This way, instead of fears, you receive encouragement, and instead of doubt, you have steadfast commitment.

Common Fear: My parents always said that the more money you have, the more you have to worry about it. What if being wealthy doesn't create the life I want?

It won't. Money is just a thing. It can't give you happiness. It can, however, buy you the freedom to spend time with your nearest and dearest. Money can buy you experiences and plane tickets to exotic places. It can't buy you health, but it can buy you regular checkups and the best treatment if illnesses occur. Money is simply a vehicle. True wealth includes financial success, a healthy happy family, a trusted partner, and great friends. How you use money will determine whether you get the life you are looking for. As you are concentrating on your wealth building, focus on your *why*. What are you building wealth for? And then each time you make a decision, ask yourself if it takes you closer to or further away from your overall goals.

Action Steps:

List all of your assets, everything you can bring to a joint venture partnership. Add value everywhere you go and start building relationships.

- We've included a Joint venture resource for you to download and fill in when presenting your investment opportunities. This is the same document I used to raise $1m
- There may be joint venture opportunities within the community so don't forget to login and active contributor there as well.

Chapter Seven

Step Seven: Leverage Everything, Leverage Now

I'm sure you've heard the saying "do what you always do and get what you've always got." Well, that applies to leverage and delegation, possibly more than any other area of life. The majority of people are employed or self-employed in a job. As a result, they have only eight hours a day to earn money. Microsoft is said to have 99,000 employees, giving Bill Gates 792,000 hours in his day to serve the world and create wealth. Do you think you could create more wealth with an extra 791,992 hours per day? If you continue working harder and trying to do it all yourself in one day, you will never create wealth or sustainable businesses.

There's a common myth that goes something like this: Wealthy people just get it done. They are great at juggling and just fitting it all in.

This is categorically not true. The really wealthy people acknowledge that a lot of their success comes from their team. The greatest business leaders of all time are fantastic at building teams of people smarter than themselves. Many of the greatest investors don't work day to day, but they employ hundreds of people. The wealthiest investors don't spend their own money but invest that of joint venture partners. If you are ever going to truly scale up and take your investing and your lifestyle to the next level, you need to master the art of leverage. Not many people decide they would like to invest in real estate because they want to give themselves more to do and more stress, yet because they never get the hang of leverage, that's exactly what ends up happening.

When you have invested all of yourself into a business to step away from the hands-on aspect, it isn't easy, and it takes a whole lot of new skills that you're going to have to learn if you don't want to make the same mistakes as others. If you're lucky, you may end up rich, but if you don't learn the skills to leverage people and money, you will never be able to create true wealth and financial abundance.

In real estate, we focus on leveraging primarily people and money.

Leverage People

To become a millionaire real estate investor, you need to master the value of your time and learn to understand what you are good at. Even before you look at creating a scalable and exciting business, just the simple buying process requires an attorney, a surveyor, a valuer, a realtor, and many more trained professionals. Automatically, we leverage those people and their skills without thinking about it because it doesn't make sense—either financially or from the point of view of time—to go through school to become a real estate lawyer just to buy houses. The return on investment just isn't worth it. Yet many people do not think twice about trying to learn carpentry or other skills to fit doors and redecorate in a bid to save time and money.

As a leader and strategic investor, your strengths are in spotting opportunities. Because of the time you have and will continue to spend on learning strategies and honing your ability to spot ways of adding value, your role should more and more become about appraising deals and investment opportunities. Spending time learning how to decorate and repair wardrobes distracts you from what you are really good at, which is structuring deals, networking, creating great businesses, and being a leader. If you got right down to it, you could probably source a fantastic investment opportunity within a few days that could easily earn you $5,000 without even trying very hard! If you spend all of your time putting furniture together to save $100, you are denying yourself the opportunity to find these deals and make more money. You are also doing the community a disservice by not providing a job opportunity when you have one.

The natural inclination is to save money when you are financially challenged and sometimes what appears to be a small job seems like a great way of saving money. But in reality—and especially if you don't have those skills—it will cost you more in the long run. Create a new habit to outsource everything you can't or don't like doing, and when you feel as if you really can't afford it, commit to spending the time you would have spent in carrying out that activity finding a profitable investment that can make you a massive return on the money you invested in great people. Leverage other people to use their knowledge and skills, and give them the opportunity to do what they are great at. Cluttering your mind and your time with these things will stunt the growth of your wealth.

Top Tip: Throughout the day, ask yourself if what you are doing has the biggest potential return on investment for your time spent. Simply put, are you using the 80/20 rule effectively and doing the things that earn eighty percent of your income? Or are you wasting time doing tasks that could be outsourced for a few dollars? Rather than thinking *how do I do it*, think *who can do it for me!*

Outsourcing can be anything from employing a full-time member of staff to buying a 'gig' on fiverr.com (watch the training videos to hear more about this) to have a small task completed for you. In most small businesses, it is administration work that keeps the owner tied to a desk and away from growing the business. Outsourcing to a lower-priced economy is a fantastic way to offload this work to a highly-qualified person in need of a job. For example, we have some virtual assistants based in the Philippines. They are all fantastic and do all kinds of work from graphic design to website design to answering the phones. They are the best earners by far in their town, and they love their work, but they cost me probably twenty percent of what it would cost to recruit from Europe or the US.

Leverage Finance

There is a startling difference between the financial habits of the wealthy and those of the poor. These habits are ingrained before we even realize it. The poor grow up thinking, "I'll buy it when I can afford it," but the wealthy think, "How can I afford it?" The poor think if they work harder, they will eventually be able to buy it. The wealthy think maybe they can borrow it from someone who already has it.

As with other assets like time, if you waited until you had enough money to buy all the properties you wanted, you would never have enough. It doesn't matter if you are sitting on millions, there will come a point when you don't have enough liquid cash to get in on a great deal because your money is currently being used. Financial leverage is the single most exciting and profitable aspect of real estate investment.

At the moment, banks will lend fifty to ninety percent of the purchase price. We are coming out of the biggest financial meltdown ever, so yes, lending criteria is a bit tighter than previously. But if you speak to a good broker, most people will be able to get a bank to give them at least seventy-five percent of the price of a house. This is incredible, and so undervalued! Once you have the property, you then leverage again and have your tenants pay your mortgage for you. And you get profit! Awesome!

Banks are just one of many ways to finance real estate. Because of its intrinsic value, getting finance for properties is so easy. Some other potential investment sources are angel investors, joint venture partners, venture capitalists, family offices, debt leverage, equity gearing—the list is endless!

As you become really experienced and tactical at leverage, you can have someone else pay for your house, have someone refurbish it, have someone else find and manage your tenants, and someone else pay the mortgage. I don't know any other wealth vehicle that will pay you to buy assets in the same way.

Start with the End in Mind—Strategy and Systems

I don't want to be a landlady. You might be surprised to hear me saying that given that I love real estate and own several million dollars' worth of property. I can see why you would be confused, but here's the thing—I love property, architecture, and deals. I love creating something that wasn't there before, and I love providing great homes. I love earning money and knowing that I've left my stamp on the world. I absolutely do *not* love managing tenants. I don't enjoy the daily monotonous tasks—checking rent in, chasing payments, liaising with builders, doing check-ins, and collecting keys. None of that interests me, and it never has. I have always been very clear on this, and so when I set the systems and processes up in my business, I made sure I wasn't included in them.

I knew from the beginning that being a landlady wasn't my goal. My goal was owning assets, creating monthly cash flow, providing great homes, and supporting the community. And my earliest goal was to extricate myself as quickly as possible. To enable this, we built a leasing agency to manage our properties and those of other landlords. In essence, this means that our houses are managed for free. More importantly, though, it means there are about ten people between my tenants and me. They get to talk to people who are great at helping them, and I get to stick to what I am good at—strategically planning the next investments and business plans. This is the very essence of beginning with the end in mind.

If you want to sell your business at some point, you need to be sure it runs well without you and that you have developed the systems and assets that give it value.

Become a Problem Solver

You don't need to make a billion dollars from one project. Just find something that helps a billion people and make $1 per person.

The most exciting part of being a real estate investor is the person we become as a result of the journey. Being a strategic, educated, and ethical investor gives you the opportunity to help hundreds of thousands of people stay in their homes, resolve financial challenges, move on, and start fresh. If they are ready to accept help and defy the traditionalists, you can help them move on as long as you have the right tools in your tool box. The strategies I've shared with you in the previous chapters are just some of the hundreds of tools I have available. As a result, I get to help thousands of people each year. The better I get, the more tools I have, and the more people I help. Subsequently, the money I make in an ethical and sustainable way makes me proud of my work and leaves legacies countrywide in communities that are better off for our presence.

The Fallacy of the Big Idea was coined years ago by British multimillionaire Felix Dennis. He shared his experience of working with budding entrepreneurs. They felt they had to reinvent the wheel and come up with 'the great idea' that would make them millions. In previous generations, this may have been true. During the industrial age, in order to make money, you had to exploit the efforts of other people to make your factory produce more or your trains go faster. These times have passed. We are now in the age of service. To earn more, we must become givers not takers. To be truly wealthy, we need to become producers and not just consumers.

The more people we serve, the greater the difference we get to make in the world. Having a big portfolio and multiple six figure plus projects in the works is great. The challenges, the learnings, and yes, the money is awesome, but it would all mean nothing to me if I didn't also know that I was providing great homes to hundreds of people, and that our team had saved people from bankruptcy, foreclosure, and breakdowns. We make a difference—and a fortune—and now it's your turn.

To become a millionaire, you don't need a great idea, and you don't need to reinvent the wheel. You just need to develop the tools to solve problems. It is in times of change and uncertainty that great innovators become great leaders. We are in perhaps in the biggest time of uncertainty ever known to the world, and the world is ready for you to stand up, create wealth, and make a difference.

Action Points

Leverage is the secret sauce that will exponentially grow your business and your wealth. Outsource everything you don't want to do and everything you are not good at. Focus solely on the roles that are income generating and need YOU.

- Check out the outsourcing guide in the Chapter 7 of the Freedom Property member's community to find affordable tasks for you to begin outsourcing immediately.
- We have added some training videos for you to start to build your team

WHAT NEXT?

It's your time to rock!

Whatever your goals and dreams if you just commit to the process, they can be yours. But you can't do it alone. So, come and join the community and get INSTANT ACCESS to:

- **Free VIP Membership** to Freedom Property Academy (http://www.freedompropertyacademy.com/book)
- **Free Video training** from Kemi featuring joint venture training, real estate strategy training, audio and video programs supporting all 7 steps updated regularly. A comprehensive set of modules and resources online.
- **Attend Live Training webinars** from Kemi and the team. Updates will be posted inside the community for the latest training events where you can grab a hot seat.
- **Join the Community –** Post questions, help others and get joint venture opportunities, joint venture partners and access to VIP only events
- **Downloads and Resources –** Get access to documents, templates and examples from all seven modules. Joint venture presentation proformas, deal structuring examples and much much more.

ONE MORE THING

I wrote this book for you. This is the book I would have loved during the first few years of my journey. I would love to hear what you think so if you leave a review on Amazon, Audible or anywhere else send me a link or screenshot at **kemi.egan@freedomacademies.com** and I have another extra special gift to thank you.

About the Author

Kemi is Co-Founder of Freedom Academies and the Freedom Property Group.

Kemi is an in demand keynote speaker, consultant and facilitator in the areas of business growth, joint ventures, real estate and personal finance. A sought after Business Growth Speaker, Author, and consultant working with Executives, SME's, Corporates and educational establishments worldwide.

Kemi is authentic, uncommonly honest and genuine. Her high energy and dynamic manner is a hit at conferences, seminars, boot camps and speaking engagements.

To Kemi about booking her to speak, consult or work with your organisation please contact her at:
kemi.egan@freedomacademies.com

Connect with me here:

www.twitter.com/KemiEgan

www.facebook.com/kemieganfreedomacademies

Made in the USA
Columbia, SC
27 November 2023

27110831R00098